PERFECT PHRASES
in Spanish
for the
HOTEL and RESTAURANT INDUSTRIES

PERFECT PHRASES
in Spanish

for the
HOTEL and
RESTAURANT
INDUSTRIES

**500+ Essential Words and Phrases
for Communicating with Spanish-Speakers**

Jean Yates

New York Chicago San Francisco Lisbon London Madrid Mexico City
Milan New Delhi San Juan Seoul Singapore Sydney Toronto

The **McGraw·Hill** Companies

Library of Congress Cataloging-in-Publication Data

Yates, Jean.
     Perfect phrases in Spanish for the hotel and restaurant industries / Jean Yates.
        p.   cm. — (Perfect phrases in Spanish)
     ISBN 0-07-149478-2 (alk. paper)
     1. Spanish language—Conversation and phrase books (for restaurant and hotel
personnel).   I. Title.

    PC4120.R4Y38   2007
    468.3'421024795—dc22   2007045528

1 2 3 4 5 6 7 8 9 10 11 12 13 14 15 16 17 18 19 20 21   DOC/DOC   0 9 8

ISBN 978-0-07-149478-6
MHID   0-07-149478-2

McGraw-Hill books are available at special quantity discounts to use as premiums and
sales promotions or for use in corporate training programs. To contact a representative,
please visit the Contact Us pages at www.mhprofessional.com.

This book is printed on acid-free paper.

The author would like to thank Gina García
for her very helpful comments.

Contents

Introduction   xi

CHAPTER 1: SPANISH BASICS   1

Greetings   1
Pleasantries   2
Family and Friends   3
The "Magic" Words   5
Telling Present Time and Using Numbers 1–12   6
Indicating Work Hours   9
Talking to More than One Person at a Time   10
Days of the Week   10
Months of the Year and Using Numbers 1–31   12
Talking About the Weather   15
Interviewing an Employee   15
  Asking for References   16
Hiring an Employee   17
Scheduling   18
Discussing Salary and Using Numbers 40+   19
  Rates of Payment   22
  Discussing Pay Periods   22
Discussing Taxes   23
Showing Appreciation for Good Work   24

Contents

Clearing Up Confusion   25

Terminating an Employee   25

Basic Questions and Answers   27

  Yes-or-No Questions   27

  Information Questions   28

CHAPTER 2: ESTABLISHING POLICIES   33

Entering and Leaving the Hotel   35

Hotel Employees   37

Dress Codes and Policies for Employees   38

Equipment and Supplies   41

Setting Priorities   42

Emergency Policies   42

Safety Precautions   44

CHAPTER 3: GENERAL INSTRUCTIONS   47

Indicating Order and Repetition of Tasks   50

Indicating Locations of Things   51

Going Places and Taking Things   52

CHAPTER 4: SPECIFIC TASKS FOR
               GUEST ROOM ATTENDANTS   55

Introducing the Guest Rooms   55

Tasks for Cleaning the Guest Rooms   56

  Cleaning the Room and Its Contents   57

  Changing the Beds   61

  Replenishing Supplies in the Room   63

Contents

Tasks for Cleaning the Bathrooms   64
Final Tasks   66
Interacting with Guests   68

CHAPTER 5: SPECIFIC TASKS FOR THE LAUNDRY UNIT   71

Introducing the Work in the Laundry   71
Operating Laundry Machines   73
The Washing Machines   73
The Dryers   78
The Pressing and Folding Machines   79
Stacking and Packing Finished Items   82
Laundry Room Maintenance   82

CHAPTER 6: SPECIFIC INSTRUCTIONS FOR KITCHEN AND FOOD SERVICE STAFF   85

Working in the Kitchen   85
Getting Ready to Work   86
Preparing Food   87
Utensils for Preparing Food   89
Cooking   90
Baking   93
Arranging Food on Plates and Garnishing   95
Emergencies   96
Kitchen Maintenance   97
Organizing the Kitchen   98
Washing Dishes   98
Disposing of Garbage   100

Contents

Food Service   102
   Room Service   102
   Banquet Setup   105
   Banquet Service   110
   Banquet Cleanup   113

CHAPTER 7: SPECIFIC TASKS FOR THE INDOOR MAINTENANCE TEAM   115

Routine Cleaning of Public Rooms   116
   Tools and Equipment   118
Keeping the Hotel in Good Repair   120
   Routine Tasks for the Maintenance Team   120
   Special Projects for the Maintenance Team   121
   Tools and Equipment   124
Pest Control   126

Appendix: Numbers   129
English-Spanish Glossary   133
Glosario español-inglés   155

Introduction

In many parts of the United States, hotels, motels, and guest houses are employing at an increasing rate Spanish-speaking housekeepers, laundry workers, kitchen and food service staff, and indoor and outdoor maintenance workers who do not speak English. This book is designed to provide such employers with simple phrases in Spanish that will enable them to communicate basic information to their employees, helping to ensure that they understand the information necessary for jobs to be done correctly, efficiently, and safely. In learning some Spanish phrases, employers often develop stronger working relationships with their employees, who are generally most appreciative of this interest.

It is very common for people who do not speak each others' languages to communicate with hand signals, gestures, or words they may have heard others say. This may lead to a certain level of mutual understanding, but it is certainly less than ideal, especially in a job setting, as it often ends in misunderstandings by both parties, can cause mishaps and bad feelings, and could even be dangerous. In this book, employers will find key words and phrases that will help them begin communicating with their Spanish-speaking employees in a clear and correct manner right from the beginning. While this is not a course in grammar or conversation, those who consistently use these words and phrases with their employees will find that they are beginning to understand and use quite a bit of Spanish, and can actually build on this foundation to continue learning the language.

How This Book Is Organized

The phrases in this book are divided into six sections. In Chapter 1, you will find general words and expressions that are used every day to say such things as *hello* and *good-bye*, *please* and *thank you*, and other common courtesies. Also in this section are the phrases that will enable you to hire and terminate help and to explain to an employee the general rules and policies of employment with you, including such topics as wages, social security payments, punctuality, and so forth. You will also find the words to help you express satisfaction or dissatisfaction with an employee's performance. In Chapter 2, you will find phrases for introducing your hotel to potential employees and establishing the basic policies regarding working there. Chapter 3 provides phrases for giving general instructions. Chapter 4 includes specific phrases for explaining to housekeeping staff how you expect things to be done in that department. Chapter 5 includes specific phrases for laundry room workers. Chapter 6 provides the vocabulary for giving instructions to kitchen and food service workers, and Chapter 7 the words and phrases for indoor maintenance workers. The two glossaries contain all the words used in the book and are arranged in alphabetical order, the first from English to Spanish, and the second from Spanish to English. In addition, there is a table of the numbers from 0 to multiple millions, for handy reference.

Vocabulary Guidelines

Throughout the book there are phrases that allow for substitutable words. When this occurs, the word that can be replaced with another is <u>underlined</u>. Then one, two, or more words that could easily replace the underlined word are presented. This feature will help you memorize the most useful phrases, and generate an unlimited number of useful sentences. An example is shown below:

This is a <u>single room</u>.	**Esta es una <u>habitación sencilla</u>.**
	(EH-stah es oo-nah ah-bee-tah-
	S'YOHN sen-SEE-yah)
double room	**habitación doble**
	(ah-bee-tah-S'YOHN
	DOH-bleh)
suite	**suite**
	(eh-SWEET)

Pronunciation Guidelines

Each phrase in Chapter 1 and Chapter 2 is printed in Spanish to the right of its equivalent English phrase, with a guide to its pronunciation written directly underneath. The symbols used are an approximation of how the words would sound if they were written in English, as illustrated below.

Vowels

To make a Spanish vowel sound, open your mouth and place your lips in position, and do not move your lips until you make the next sound.

Spanish Spelling	**Approximate Pronunciation**
a	ah
e	eh
i	ee
o	oh
u	oo

Introduction

To make a vowel combination, begin with the first vowel, then move your lips into the position of the second.

ai	eye
ei	ay (like the *ei* in *weight*)
oi	oy
ui	wee
ia	yah
ie	yeh
io	yoh
iu	yoo
au	ah'oo
eu	eh'oo
ua	wah
ue	weh
uo	woh

Consonants

b	b
ca / co / cu	kah / koh / koo
ce / ci	seh / see
d (to begin a word)	d
d (after a vowel)	th (as in *brother*)
f	f
ga / go / gu	gah / goh / goo
ge / gi	heh / hee
h	silent (like the *h* in *honest*)
j	h

la / le / li / lo / lu	lah / leh / lee / loh / loo
al / el / il / ol / ul	adl / edl / eedl / odl / udl
ll	y / j
m	m
n	n
n (before c / g)	ng (like the *ng* in *finger*)
ña / ñe / ñi / ño / ñu	n'yah / n'yeh / n'yee / n'yoh / n'yoo
p	p
que / qui	keh / kee
r (at the beginning)	rrr (trilled)
r (between vowels)	d / tt / dd
bari	body
beri	Betty
biri	beady
ora	oughtta
vuru	voodoo
rr	rrr (trilled)
s	s
t	t
v	b
x	ks
y	y / j
z	s

Syllables

As a general rule, in the transcription each syllable that is printed in lower case letters should be pronounced with the same tone and length, and the syllable printed in capital letters should be emphasized, by saying it a little louder and longer than the others. For example, the word **bueno**, which means *good*, is represented as follows:

good   **bueno**
                                       (B'WEH-noh)

How to Get the Most Out of This Book

There are many ways that you can help build your Spanish vocabulary:

- Use the pronunciation guidelines provided, but also listen to your employees and try to copy their pronunciation.
- Customize your phrases by substituting words with other words from the lists provided, and also with new words you may learn from your employee. Words that are underlined can be substituted with words from the alphabetical lists provided in Part 7.
- Keep a notebook—ask your employee to say or write down problematical words or expressions; then, if you cannot find the word in this book, seek help from a dictionary or a bilingual speaker.
- To learn new words from your employee, begin right away by memorizing the following question:

How do you say _____   **¿Cómo se dice _____en español?**
   in Spanish?   (KOH-moh seh DEE-seh _____en
                                eh-spahn-YOHL)

The words you get as answers to your question can be added to your notebook to help you remember them.

Cultural Guidelines

In most Spanish-speaking countries, there are three ways to say *you*: **tú**, to a person you generally socialize with; **usted**, to any other person, including a person you work for or who works for you, and **ustedes**, to two or more people whom you are talking to at the same time. The phrases in this book are given in the **usted** form, and instructions are also provided for changing these to the plural **ustedes** form. This will ensure that you are speaking to your employees in a respectful manner that will certainly be appreciated. Employees will also respond to you with this form.

Some Hispanic cultures have a more relaxed concept of time than that generally accepted in the United States. You will need to make it clear that arriving on time and on the agreed day(s), especially for work, is very important in this country, and that if an emergency arises that causes an employee to be late or unable to work, you expect to be informed right away.

You may want to have some idea about the family situations of your employees, as family is generally very important in Hispanic culture. Your workers may be supporting a number of family members both here and back home. Be sure to make clear to those who work for you what your policies are for time off for family emergencies and celebrations as well as for personal illness.

Chapter 1

Spanish Basics

Exchanging pleasantries and greetings with your Spanish-speaking employees is a great way to begin to build a stronger working relationship.

Greetings

Hello.	**Hola.**
	(OH-lah)
Good morning.	**Buenos días.**
	(B'WEH-nohs DEE-ahs)
Good afternoon.	**Buenas tardes.**
	(B'WEH-nahs TAR-thess)
Good evening.	**Buenas noches.**
	(B'WEH-nahs NOH-chess)
Good night.	**Buenas noches.**
	(B'WEH-nahs NOH-chess)
Good-bye.	**Adiós.**
	(ah-TH'YOHS)

See you later.	**Hasta luego.**
	(AH-stahl WEH-goh)
Have a nice day.	**Que le vaya bien.** (*lit*: May all go well
	for you—to someone who is
	leaving)
	(keh leh bah-yah B'YEN)

In Spanish sometimes you need to change your greeting, depending on whether you are speaking to a male or a female and also when you speak to several people together. In the examples below, you'll see four ways to say "Welcome":

Welcome. (to a male)	**Bienvenido.**
	(b'yen beh-NEE-thoh)
Welcome. (to a female)	**Bienvenida.**
	(b'yen-beh-NEE-thah)
Welcome. (to an all-male or mixed group)	**Bienvenidos.**
	(b'yen-beh-NEE-thohs)
Welcome. (to an all-female group)	**Bienvenidas.**
	(b'yen-beh-NEE-thahs)

Pleasantries

Just as "Hi, how are you?" is usually the first thing we say to each other in English, its equivalent in Spanish is the most usual greeting.

How are you?	**¿Cómo está?**
	(KOHM-weh-STAH)

To say the same thing to more than one person, just add **n** to **está**, making **están**:

How are you (all)?	**¿Cómo están?**
	(KOHM-weh-STAHN)

Here are some stock answers:

Fine, thank you.	**Bien, gracias.**
	(B'YEN GRAHS-yahs)
So-so.	**Regular.**
	(reh-goo-LAHR)
	Más o menos. (*lit*: more or less)
	(MAHS oh MEH-nos)
Not well.	**Mal.**
	(MAHL)

Family and Friends

"Family first" is an important concept in Hispanic culture, and asking about the health of family members is one way of showing that you understand and appreciate this.

Use the following formula to ask about one person:

How is your <u>mother</u>?	**¿Cómo está su <u>mamá</u>?**
	(KOHM-weh-STAH soo mah-MAH)

Just substitute any of the following words to ask about others:

father	**papá**
	(pah-PAH)
husband	**esposo**
	(eh-SPOH-soh)
wife	**esposa**
	(eh-SPOH-sah)
sister	**hermana**
	(ehr-MAH-nah)
brother	**hermano**
	(ehr-MAH-noh)
son	**hijo**
	(EE-hoh)
daughter	**hija**
	(EE-hah)

To inquire about more than one person at a time, just add **s** to **su**, another **s** to make the word plural, and add **n** to **está**:

How are your <u>parents</u>?	**¿Cómo están sus <u>papás</u>?**
	(KOHM-weh-STAHN soos pah-PAHS)
children	**hijos**
	(EE-hohs)
daughters	**hijas**
	(EE-hahs)
sisters and brothers	**hermanos**
	(ehr-MAH-nohs)
sisters	**hermanas**
	(ehr-MAH-nahs)

While we're on the subject of people important to us, let's include a few more who we can't do without:

friend (male)	**amigo**
	(ah-MEE-goh)
friend (female)	**amiga**
	(ah-MEE-gah)
boyfriend	**novio**
	(NOH-b'yoh)
girlfriend	**novia**
	(NOH-b'yah)
boss (male)	**patrón / jefe**
	(pah-TROHN) / (HEH-feh)
boss (female)	**patrona / jefa**
	(pah-TROH-nah) / (HEH-fah)
neighbor (male)	**vecino**
	(beh-SEE-noh)
neighbor (female)	**vecina**
	(beh-SEE-nah)

These words can also be made plural, by adding **s** (or **es** in the case of **patrón**). (It's probably not a good idea to make **novio** or **novia** plural.)

The "Magic" Words

These are the essential words for showing courtesy and respect. Memorize these right away.

Please.	**Por favor.**
	(por fah-BOR)
Thank you.	**Gracias.**
	(GRAH-s'yahs)
You're welcome.	**De nada.**
	(deh NAH-thah)
Excuse me.	**Disculpe.**
	(dees-KOOL-peh)
I'm sorry.	**Lo siento.**
	(loh S'YEN-toh)

Telling Present Time and Using Numbers 1–12

In the following section, you will find phrases for asking and telling the time. The numbers from 1–12, which you will need for other purposes as well, are introduced here.

What time is it?	**¿Qué hora es?**
	(KEH OH-rah ess)

This question is answered for *one o'clock* by the phrase:

It's one o'clock.	**Es la una.**
	(ess lah OO-nah)

For all other hours, use the following phrase, inserting a number between two and twelve:

Spanish Basics

It's two o'clock.	**Son las <u>dos</u>.**
	(sohn lahs DOHS)
three	**tres**
	(TRESS)
four	**cuatro**
	(K'WAH-troh)
five	**cinco**
	(SEENG-koh)
six	**seis**
	(SACE) (rhymes with *face*)
seven	**siete**
	(S'YEH-teh)
eight	**ocho**
	(OH-choh)
nine	**nueve**
	(N'WEH-beh)
ten	**diez**
	(D'YESS)
eleven	**once**
	(OHN-seh)
twelve	**doce**
	(DOH-seh)

For times in between the hours, use the following expressions:

It's one-fifteen.	**Es la una y cuarto.**
	(ess lah OO-nah ee K'WAHR-toh)
It's two-thirty.	**Son las dos y media.**
	(sohn lahs DOHS ee MEH-th'yah)

It's three-forty-five.

Son las tres y cuarenta y cinco.

(sohn lahs TRESS ee kwah-REN-tah

ee SEENG-koh)

You can express *noon* and *midnight* as follows:

It's twelve o'clock noon.

Es mediodía.

(ess meh-th'yoh-DEE-ah)

It's midnight.

Es medianoche.

(ess meh-th'yah NOH-cheh)

To indicate *morning*, add **de la mañana** to any hour:

It's ten A.M.

Son las diez de la mañana.

(sohn lahs D'YESS deh lah

mah-N'YAH-nah)

For afternoon or evening, add **de la tarde**:

It's four P.M.

Son las cuatro de la tarde.

(sohn lahs K'WAH-troh deh lah

TAHR-deh)

For night, add **de la noche**:

It's nine P.M.

Son las nueve de la noche.

(sohn lahs N'WEH-beh deh lah

NOH-cheh)

Indicating Work Hours

When you want someone to be somewhere or to do something at a particular time, use the following time expressions. Note that *one o'clock* is again slightly different from all the others:

at one o'clock	**a la una**
	(ah lah OO-nah)
at two o'clock	**a las dos**
	(ah lahs DOHS)
at four-thirty	**a las cuatro y media**
	(ah lahs K'WAH-troh ee MEH-th'yah)

The concept of time may be a little fuzzier in Hispanic culture. The following expressions will indicate that you mean "gringo" time, that is, "on the dot." (And don't forget the "magic" **por favor**!)

Come tomorrow.	**Venga mañana.**
	(BENG-gah mah-N'YAH-nah)
Be here at seven.	**Esté aquí a las siete.**
	(eh-STEH ah-KEE ah lahs S'YEH-teh)
on the dot	**en punto**
	(en POON-toh)
Be on time.	**Sea puntual.**
	(SEH-ah poon-TWAHL)
Come early.	**Venga temprano.**
	(BENG-gah tem-PRAH-noh)

Don't be late.	**No venga tarde.**
	(NOH BENG-gah TAHR-deh)
You will be finished at five o'clock.	**Terminará a las cinco.**
	(tehr-mee-nah-RAH ah lahs SEENG-koh)

Talking to More than One Person at a Time

Just as before, to give instructions to a group of people, just add **n** to the main word:

Come. (to one person)	**Venga.**
	(BENG-gah)
Come. (to two or more people)	**Vengan.**
	(BENG-gahn)
Be here. (to one person)	**Esté aquí.**
	(eh-STEH ah-KEE)
Be here. (to two or more people)	**Estén aquí.**
	(eh-STEN ah-KEE)

Days of the Week

If you look at a Spanish calendar, you will see that the extreme left-hand column is for Monday, rather than Sunday, as in the North American version. Sunday is put in the extreme right-hand column, putting the weekend days together. Most workers expect a free day a week, not necessarily on a weekend. This day is often referred to by workers as **mi día** (*my day*).

Spanish Basics

What day is today?	**¿Qué día es hoy?**
	(KEH DEE-ah ess OY)
Today is <u>Monday</u>.	**Hoy es <u>lunes</u>.**
	(OY ess LOO-ness)
Tomorrow is <u>Tuesday</u>.	**Mañana es <u>martes</u>.**
	(mah-N'YAH-nah ess MAHR-tess)
Wednesday	**miércoles**
	(M'YEHR-koh-less)
Thursday	**jueves**
	(H'WEH-bess)
Friday	**viernes**
	(B'YER-ness)
Saturday	**sábado**
	(SAH-bah-thoh)
Sunday	**domingo**
	(doh-MEENG-goh)

To indicate a day in the future, add **el** before the name of the day:

Be here on Monday.	**Esté aquí el lunes.**
	(eh-STEH ah-KEE el LOO-ness)

To indicate *always on that day* add **los** before the name of the day:

Come on Mondays.	**Venga los lunes.**
	(BENG-gah lohs LOO-ness)
Come every day.	**Venga todos los días.**
	(BENG-gah TOH-thos lohs DEE-ahs)

Don't come on Sundays.

No venga los domingos.
(NOH BENG-gah lohs
doh-MEENG-gohs)

Months of the Year and Using Numbers 1–31

Did you notice that the days of the week are not capitalized in Spanish? It's the same with the months. Also, when giving the date in abbreviated form, it is exactly the opposite from English. In other words, 3/9/07 in English would be March 9, 2007. In Spanish it would be the 3rd of September, 2007. Let's look at how these dates are written and said.

What's the date?

¿Cuál es la fecha?
(K'WAHL ess lah FEH-chah)

It's the first of January.

Es el primero de enero.
(ess el pree-MEH-roh deh
eh-NEH-roh)

After "the first" day, dates are given in cardinal numbers, as in "the 'two' of January," "the 'three' of January," and so forth. The following examples use all of the months, and numbers up to thirty-one.

It's the second of January.

Es el dos de enero.
(ess el DOHS deh eh-NEH-roh)

the third of February

el tres de febrero
(el TRESS deh feh-BREH-roh)

the fourth of March

el cuatro de marzo
(el K'WAH-troh deh MAHR-soh)

the fifth of April

el cinco de abril

(el SEENG-koh deh ah-BREEL)

the sixth of May

el seis de mayo

(el SACE deh MAH-yoh)

the seventh of June

el siete de junio

(el S'YEH-teh deh HOON-yoh)

the eighth of July

el ocho de julio

(el OH-choh deh HOOL-yoh)

the ninth of August

el nueve de agosto

(el N'WEH-beh deh
    ah-GOH-stoh)

the tenth of September

el diez de septiembre

(el D'YESS deh sep-T'YEM-breh)

the eleventh of October

el once de octubre

(el OHN-seh deh
    ohk-TOO-breh)

the twelfth of November

el doce de noviembre

(el DOH-seh deh
    noh-B'YEM-breh)

the thirteenth of December

el trece de diciembre

(el TREH-seh deh
    dee-S'YEM-breh)

the fourteenth

el catorce

(el kah-TOR-seh)

the fifteenth

el quince

(el KEEN-seh)

the sixteenth

el dieciséis

(el d'yes-ee-SACE)

the seventeenth

el diecisiete

(el d'yes-ee-S'YEH-teh)

the eighteenth	**el dieciocho**
	(el d'yes-YOH-choh)
the nineteenth	**el diecinueve**
	(el d'yes-ee-N'WEH-beh)
the twentieth	**el veinte**
	(el BAYN-teh)
the twenty-first	**el veintiuno**
	(el bayn-T'YOO-noh)
the twenty-second	**el veintidós**
	(el bayn-tee-DOHS)
the twenty-third	**el veintitrés**
	(el bayn-tee-TRESS)
the twenty-fourth	**el veinticuatro**
	(el bayn-tee-K'WAH-troh)
the twenty-fifth	**el veinticinco**
	(el bayn-tee-SEENG-koh)
the twenty-sixth	**el veintiséis**
	(el bayn-tee-SACE)
the twenty-seventh	**el veintisiete**
	(el bayn-tee-S'YEH-teh)
the twenty-eighth	**el veintiocho**
	(el bayn-T'YOH-choh)
the twenty-ninth	**el veintinueve**
	(el bayn-tee-N'WEH-beh)
the thirtieth	**el treinta**
	(el TRAYN-tah)
the thirty-first	**el treinta y uno**
	(el TRAYN-tah ee OO-noh)

Talking About the Weather

The following are the most common expressions.

How's the weather?	**¿Qué tiempo hace?**
	(KEH T'YEM-poh AH-seh)
It's fine.	**Hace buen tiempo.**
	(AH-seh B'WEHN T'YEM-poh)
It's hot.	**Hace calor.**
	(AH-seh kah-LOR)
It's cold.	**Hace frío.**
	(AH-seh FREE-oh)
It's raining.	**Está lloviendo.**
	(eh-STAH yoh-B'YEN-doh)
It's snowing.	**Está nevando.**
	(eh-STAH neh-BAHN-doh)
It's windy.	**Hace viento.**
	(AH-seh B'YEN-toh)
It's sunny.	**Hace sol.**
	(AH-seh SOHL)
It's cloudy.	**Está nublado.**
	(eh-STAH noo-BLAH-thoh)
There's a storm.	**Hay una tormenta.**
	(EYE oo-nah tor-MEN-tah)

Interviewing an Employee

These are the phrases for learning the most basic information about your prospective employees.

What's your name?	**¿Cuál es su nombre?**
	(K'WAHL ess soo NOHM-breh)
Where are you from?	**¿De dónde es?**
	(deh THOHN-deh ess)
Where do you live?	**¿Dónde vive?**
	(DOHN-deh BEE-beh)
How long have you been here?	**¿Hace cuánto que vive aquí?**
	(AH-seh K'WAHN-toh keh BEE-beh ah-KEE)
Where did you work before?	**¿Dónde trabajó antes?**
	(DOHN-deh trah-bah-HOH AHN-tess)
What kind of work did you do?	**¿Qué tipo de trabajo hizo?**
	(KEH TEE-poh deh trah-BAH-hoh EE-soh)
Do you have any experience in hotel work?	**¿Ha trabajado en un hotel alguna vez?**
	(ah trah-bah-HAH-thoh en oon oh-TELL ahl-goo-nah BESS)
Have you worked as a cook before?	**¿Ha trabajado como cocinero alguna vez?**
	(ah trah-bah-HAH-thoh koh-moh koh-see-neh-roh ahl-goo-nah BESS)

Asking for References

Notice that the question about contacting "her" is exactly the same question about contacting "you" when you are speaking to a female.

Likewise, the question about "him" is the same as the one about "you" when you are speaking to a male.

Can you give me a reference?	**¿Me puede dar una referencia?**
	(meh PWEH-theh dahr oo-nah reh-feh-REN-s'yah)
How can I contact her?	**¿Cómo la puedo contactar?**
	(KOH-moh lah PWEH-thoh kohn-tahk-TAHR)
How can I contact him?	**¿Cómo lo puedo contactar?**
	(KOH-moh loh PWEH-thoh kohn-tahk-TAHR)
How can I contact you? (to a female)	**¿Cómo la puedo contactar?**
	(KOH-moh lah PWEH-thoh kohn-tahk-TAHR)
How can I contact you? (to a male)	**¿Cómo lo puedo contactar?**
	(KOH-moh loh PWEH-thoh kohn-tahk-TAHR)

Hiring an Employee

Here are some basic phrases that will help you establish a relationship with a new employee.

You're hired. (to a female)	**Usted está contratada.**
	(oo-STED eh-STAH kohn-trah-TAH-thah)
You're hired. (to a male)	**Usted está contratado.**
	(oo-STED eh-STAH kohn-trah-TAH-thoh)

You're hired. (to a group)	**Ustedes están contratados.**
	(oo-STEH-thehs eh-STAN
	kohn-trah-TAH-thohs)

Scheduling

Here are some phrases that will help you establish days and hours of work. To substitute different days and times, find the suitable words on the previous pages.

Can you come . . .	**¿Puede venir...**
	(PWEH-theh beh-NEER)
every day?	**todos los días?**
	(TOH-thohs lohs DEE-ahs)
every week?	**cada semana?**
	(KAH-thah seh-MAH-nah)
from Monday through Friday?	**de lunes a viernes?**
	(de LOO-ness ah B'YEHR-ness)
once a week?	**una vez a la semana?**
	(oo-nah BESS ah lah
	seh-MAH-nah)
on Monday<u>s</u>?	**los lune<u>s</u>?**
	(lohs LOO-ness)
twice a week?	**dos veces a la semana?**
	(DOHS BEH-sess ah lah
	seh-MAH-nah)
once a month?	**una vez al mes?**
	(oo-nah BESS ahl MESS)
twice a month?	**dos veces al mes?**
	(DOHS BEH-sess ahl MESS)

four hours a day?	**cuatro horas al día?**
	(K'WAH troh OH-rahs ahl DEE-ah)
thirty hours a week?	**treinta horas a la semana?**
	(TRAYN-tah OH-rahs ah lah seh-MAH-nah)

Discussing Salary and Using Numbers 40+

It's important to establish how you will pay your employee right at the beginning. Review the numbers between one and thirty-one on page 129. Higher numbers are introduced below.

Your wages will be . . .	**Su sueldo será...**
	(soo SWELL-doh seh-RAH)
eight dollars an hour	**ocho dólares por hora**
	(OH-choh DOH-lah-ress por OH-rah)
sixteen dollars for two hours	**dieciséis dólares por dos horas**
	(d'yes-ee-SACE DOH-lah-ress por DOHS OH-rahs)
forty-five	**cuarenta y cinco**
	(k'wah-REN-tah ee SEENG-koh)
fifty	**cincuenta**
	(seeng-K'WEN-tah)
sixty	**sesenta**
	(seh-SEN-tah)
seventy	**setenta**
	(seh-TEN-tah)

19

eighty	**ochenta**
	(oh-CHEN-tah)
ninety	**noventa**
	(noh-BEN-tah)
one hundred	**cien**
	(S'YEN)
one hundred (and) fifty	**ciento cincuenta**
	(S'YEN-toh seeng-K'WEN-tah)
two hundred	**doscientos**
	(dohs-YEN-tohs)
three hundred	**trescientos**
	(tress-YEN-tohs)
four hundred	**cuatrocientos**
	(k'wah-troh S'YEN-tohs)
five hundred	**quinientos**
	(keen-YEN-tohs)
six hundred	**seiscientos**
	(say-S'YEN-tohs)
seven hundred	**setecientos**
	(seh-teh-S'YEN-tohs)
eight hundred	**ochocientos**
	(oh-choh-S'YEN-tohs)
nine hundred	**novecientos**
	(noh-beh-S'YEN-tohs)
one thousand	**mil**
	(MEEL)
two thousand	**dos mil**
	(DOHS MEEL)

You may have noticed that the numbers sixteen to nineteen are each written as one word (**dieciséis**, **diecisiete**, etc.) even though their literal meaning is "ten and six," "ten and seven," etc. The same is true for the numbers twenty-one to twenty-nine: **veintiuno** ("twenty and one"), **veintidós** ("twenty and two"), etc. Beginning with the thirties, and up to ninety-nine, similar combinations are written as three words:

thirty-one	**treinta y uno**
	(TRAYN-tah ee oo-noh)
forty-two	**cuarenta y dos**
	(k'wah-REN-tah ee DOHS)
fifty-three	**cincuenta y tres**
	(seeng-K'WEN-tah ee TRESS)
sixty-four	**sesenta y cuatro**
	(seh-SEN-tah ee K'WAH-troh)
seventy-five	**setenta y cinco**
	(seh-TEN-tah ee SEENG-koh)
eighty-six	**ochenta y seis**
	(oh-CHEN-tah ee SACE)
ninety-seven	**noventa y nueve**
	(noh-BEN-tah ee N'WEH-beh)

The **y** (*and*) is important in these combinations. In contrast, while we often use *and* with hundreds in English, **y** is never used with hundreds in Spanish:

one hundred (and) ten	**ciento diez**
	(S'YEN-toh D'YES)

four hundred (and) sixty	**cuatrocientos sesenta**
	(K'WAH-troh-S'YEN-tohs seh-SEN-tah)
five hundred (and) seventy-five	**quinientos setenta y cinco**
	(keen-YEN-tohs seh-TEN-tah ee SEENG-koh)

Rates of Payment

The following phrases tell how to express "per" a period of time.

per hour	**por hora**
	(por OH-rah)
per day	**por día**
	(por DEE-ah)
per week	**por semana**
	(por seh-MAH-nah)
per month	**por mes**
	(por MESS)
for the completed job	**por el trabajo completado**
	(por el trah-BAH-hoh kohm-pleh-TAH-thoh)

Discussing Pay Periods

Making this clear at the beginning will help avoid misunderstandings.

I'll pay you . . .	**Le pagaré...**
	(leh pah-gah-REH)
at the end of each day.	**al fin de cada día.**
	(ahl FEEN deh KAH-thah DEE-ah)

at the end of the week.	**al fin de la semana.**
	(ahl FEEN deh lah seh-MAH-nah)
by check.	**con cheque.**
	(kohn CHEH-keh)
in cash.	**en efectivo.**
	(en eh-fek-TEE-boh)
We cannot pay you . . .	**No le podemos pagar...**
	(NOH leh poh-THEH-mos pah-GAHR)
in advance.	**por adelantado.**
	(por ah-theh-lahn-TAH-thoh)

Discussing Taxes

The phrases in this section will help you make it clear whether you wish to pay your employee's taxes or if you expect him to pay his own.

We will pay your Social Security taxes.	**Nosotros pagaremos sus impuestos de Seguridad Social.**
	(noh-SOH-trohs pah-gah-REH-mohs soos eem-pweh-stohs deh seh-goo-ree-THAD soh-S'YAHL)
You must pay your own Social Security taxes.	**Usted debe pagar sus propios impuestos de Seguridad Social.**
	(oo-STED deh-beh pah-GAHR soos PROH-p'yohs eem-pweh-stohs deh seh-goo-ree-THAD soh-S'YAHL)

You must pay your own income taxes. **Usted debe pagar los impuestos por sus ingresos.**

(oo-STED deh-beh pah-GAHR lohs eem-pweh-stohs por soos een-GREH-sohs)

I will help you with the documents. **Yo lo ayudaré con los documentos.**

(YOH loh ah-yoo-thah-REH kohn lohs doh-koo-MEN-tohs)

I cannot help you with the documents. **No puedo ayudarlo con los documentos.**

(NOH PWEH-thoh ah-yoo-THAR-loh kohn lohs doh-koo-MEN-tohs)

Showing Appreciation for Good Work

These are the phrases everyone likes to hear.

You did a good job. **Ha hecho buen trabajo.**

(ah EH-choh B'WEN trah-BAH-hoh)

You did a great job. **Hizo el trabajo muy bien.**

(EE-soh el trah-BAH-hoh M'WEE B'YEN)

You are punctual. **Usted es muy puntual.**

(oo-STED ess m'wee poon-TWAHL)

I'm happy with your work. **Me gusta su trabajo.**

(meh GOO-stah soo trah-BAH-hoh)

I'm raising your salary. **Voy a aumentar su sueldo.**

(boy ah ah'oo-men-TAHR soo SWELL-doh)

I am paying you extra today. **Hoy le doy algo extra.**

(OY leh doy ahl-goh EK-strah)

Clearing Up Confusion

Be sure to tell your employees what to do if they have a problem or an emergency situation.

Call me if you cannot come.	**Llámeme si no puede venir.**
	(YAH-meh-meh see noh PWEH-theh beh-NEER)
In an emergency, call me.	**Si hay una emergencia, llámeme.**
	(see EYE oo-nah eh-mehr-HEN-s'yah YAH-meh-meh)
My telephone number is 202-769-5416.	**Mi teléfono es dos cero dos, siete seis nueve, cinco cuatro uno seis.**
	(mee teh-LEH-foh-noh ess DOHS SEH-roh DOHS S'YEH-teh SACE N'WEH-beh SEENG-koh K'WAH-troh oo-noh SACE)
Tell me if you have a problem.	**Dígame si tiene algún problema.**
	(DEE-gah-meh see T'YEH-neh ahl-goon proh-BLEH-mah)
Tell me if you do not understand.	**Dígame si no entiende.**
	(DEE-gah-meh see NOH en-T'YEN-deh)

Terminating an Employee

These are the words nobody wants to hear, but sometimes they are necessary.

I no longer need you. (to a male)	**Ya no lo necesito.**
	(YAH noh loh neh-seh-SEE-toh)

I no longer need you. (to a female)	**Ya no la necesito.** (YAH noh lah neh-seh-SEE-toh)
You are fired. (to a male)	**Usted está despedido.** (oo-STED eh-STAH dess-peh-THEE-thoh)
You are fired. (to a female)	**Usted está despedida.** (oo-STED eh-STAH dess-peh-THEE-thah)
Because . . .	**Porque...** (POR-keh)
you didn't do the job well.	**no hizo bien el trabajo.** (NOH EE-soh B'YEN el trah-BAH-hoh)
you didn't come when I expected you.	**no vino cuando yo la (lo) esperaba.** (NOH BEE-noh k'wahn-doh yoh lah [loh] eh-speh-RAH-bah)
you never came on time.	**nunca llegó a tiempo**. (NOONG-kah yeh-GOH ah T'YEM-poh)
you work too slowly.	**trabaja muy lento.** (trah-BAH-hah m'wee LEN-toh)
you don't have the necessary skills.	**no tiene las habilidades necesarias.** (NOH T'YEH-neh lahs ah-beel-ee-THAH-thess neh-seh-SAHR-yahs)
you didn't follow instructions.	**no siguió las instrucciones.** (NOH see-G'YOH lahs een-strook-S'YOH-ness)

you broke a lot of things.	**rompió muchas cosas.**
	(rohm-P'YOH MOO-chahs
	KOH-sahs)
you don't get along with anybody.	**no se lleva bien con nadie.**
	(NOH seh YEH-bah B'YEN kohn
	NAH-th'yeh).
you have a bad attitude.	**tiene mala actitud.**
	(T'YEH-neh MAH-lah
	ahk-tee-TOOD)

Basic Questions and Answers

In this section you will learn how to form *yes-or-no* questions as well as those that begin with question words like *who, where, when,* etc. Typical answers are also provided.

Yes-or-No *Questions*

A *yes-or-no* (**sí o no**) question in Spanish is made by pronouncing a statement as a question. For example:

End a statement on the same tone you began on.

You have the money.	**Tiene el dinero.**
	(T'YEH-neh el dee-NEH-roh)

End a question on a tone higher than the one you began on.

Do you have the money?	**¿Tiene el dinero?**
	(T'YEH-neh el dee-NEH-roh)

It would be especially polite to include the person's name in answering this type of question:

Yes, Carlos.	**Sí, Carlos.**
	(SEE KAHR-lohs)
No, Sylvia.	**No, Sylvia.**
	(NOH SEEL-b'yah)
Maybe.	**Quizás.**
	(kee-SAHS)
It depends.	**Depende.**
	(de-PEN-deh)
God willing!	**¡Ojalá!**
	(oh-ha-LAH)

Information Questions

The following general questions and possible answers are included to help you request or provide information.

Who . . . ?	**¿Quién?**
	(K'YEN)
I	**yo**
	(YOH)
you	**usted**
	(oo-STED)
he	**él**
	(el)
she	**ella**
	(EH-yah)

we (in a mixed or all-male combination)	**nosotros** (noh-SOH-trohs)
we (when both or all are female)	**nosotras** (noh-SOH-trahs)
you all	**ustedes** (oo-STEH-thes)
they	**ellos** (EH-yohs)
they	**ellas** (EH-yahs)
With whom?	**¿Con quién?** (kohn K'YEN)
with me	**conmigo** (kohn-MEE-goh)
with <u>you</u>	**con <u>usted</u>** (kohn oo-STED)
him	**él** (el)
her	**ella** (EH-yah)
them	**ellos** (EH-yohs)
Whose is it?	**¿De quién es?** (deh K'YEN ess)
It's mine.	**Es mío.** (ess MEE-oh)
It's yours / his / hers / theirs	**Es suyo.** (ess SOO-yoh)

What is it?	**¿Qué es?**
	(KEH ess)
It's <u>this</u>.	**Es <u>esto</u>.**
	(ess EH-stoh)
that	**eso**
	(EH-soh)
Where is it?	**¿Dónde está?**
	(DOHN-deh eh-STAH)
It's <u>here</u>.	**Está <u>aquí</u>.**
	(eh-STAH ah-KEE)
there	**ahí**
	(ah-EE)
over there	**allí**
	(ah-YEE)
Where are you going?	**¿Adónde va?**
	(ah-THOHN-deh bah)
I'm going <u>home</u>	**Voy <u>a casa</u>.**
	(BOY ah KAH-sah)
to the fourth floor.	**al cuarto piso.**
	(ahl KWAR-toh PEE-soh)
When . . . ?	**¿Cuándo?**
	(KWAHN-doh)
now	**ahora**
	(ah-OH-rah)
later	**más tarde**
	(MAHS TAHR-deh)
soon	**pronto**
	(PROHN-toh)
always	**siempre**
	(S'YEM-preh)

never	**nunca**
	(NOONG-kah)
Until when?	**¿Hasta cuándo?**
	(ah-stah KWAHN-doh)
Until Monday.	**Hasta el lunes.**
	(ah-stah el LOO-ness)
Until three o'clock.	**Hasta las tres.**
	(ah-stah lahs TRESS)
How . . . ?	**¿Cómo?**
	(KOH-moh)
Like this. / Like that.	**Así.**
	(ah-SEE)
For how long?	**¿Por cuánto tiempo?**
	(por K'WAHN-toh T'YEM-poh)
For two hours.	**Por dos horas.**
	(por dohs OH-rahs)
A few minutes.	**Unos pocos minutos.**
	(oo-nohs poh-kohs mee-NOO-tohs)
How many are there?	**¿Cuántos hay?**
	(K'WAHN-tohs EYE)
There is one.	**Hay uno.**
	(eye OO-noh)
There are two.	**Hay dos.**
	(eye DOHS)
There are a lot.	**Hay muchos.**
	(eye MOO-chohs)
a few	**unos pocos**
	(oo-nohs POH-kohs)

How much is it?

¿Cuánto es?

(K'WAHN-toh ess)

    It's <u>twenty</u> dollars.

    Son <u>veinte</u> dólares.

    (sohn BAYN-teh DOH-lah-ress)

    It's <u>a lot</u>.

    Es <u>mucho</u>.

    (ess MOO-choh)

    only a little

    muy poco

    (m'wee poh-koh)

Chapter 2

Establishing Policies

The following phrases will help you acquaint your new employees with their workplace.

The word for hotel in Spanish is **hotel**—but it is pronounced differently than in English. In Spanish the letter **h** is always silent—like the *h* in *honest*.

hotel	**hotel**
	(oh-TELL)
This is a five-star hotel.	**Este es un hotel de cinco estrellas.**
	(EH-steh es oon oh-TELL deh SEENG-koh eh-STREH-yahs)
four	**cuatro**
	(KWAH-troh)
three	**tres**
	(TRESS)
We have three-hundred guest rooms.	**Tenemos trescientas habitaciones para huéspedes.**
	(teh-neh-mohs tress-YEN-tahs ah-bee-tahs-YOH-ness pah-rah WESS-peh-thess)

a garage with two-hundred parking spaces	**un garaje con doscientos espacios para estacionamiento.**
	(oon gah-RAH-heh kohn dohs-YEN-tohs eh-spahs-yohs pah-rah eh-stah-s'yoh-nahm-YEN-toh)
a gym	**un gimnasio**
	(oon heem-NAH-s'yoh)
a swimming pool	**una piscina**
	(oo-nah pee-SEE-nah)
Our guests expect . . .	**Nuestros huéspedes exigen...**
	(n'weh-strohs WESS-peh-thess ek-SEE-hen)
courteous service	**servicio con cortesía**
	(sehr-BEE-s'yoh kohn kor-teh-SEE-ah)
prompt	**puntual**
	(poon-TWAHL)
efficient	**eficiente**
	(eh-feese-YEN-teh)
clean rooms	**habitaciones limpias**
	(ah-bee-tahs-YOH-ness LEEMP-yahs)
clean public areas	**áreas públicas limpias**
	(AH-reh-ahs POOB-lee-kahs LEEMP-yahs)
good food	**comida buena**
	(koh-MEE-thah BWEH-nah)
healthy	**saludable**
	(sah-loo-THAH-bleh)

security	**seguridad**
	(seh-goo-ree-THAD)
privacy	**privacidad**
	(pree-bah-see-THAD)
V.I.P. service	**servicio especial**
	(sehr-BEE-s'yoh eh-speh-S'YAHL)

Entering and Leaving the Hotel

Here are phrases that specify where and how employees should enter and leave the premises of the hotel.

When you arrive for work . . .	**Cuando usted llegue a trabajar...**
	(kwahn-doh oo-STED YEH-geh ah trah-bah-HAR)
Come in the front door	**Entre por la puerta principal.**
	(EN-treh por lah P'WEHR-tah preen-see-PAHL)
the back door	**la puerta de atrás**
	(lah P'WEHR-tah deh ah-TRAHS)
the service entrance	**la entrada de servicio**
	(lah en-TRAH-thah deh sehr-BEE-s'yoh)
Use your key to open the door	**Use su llave para abrir la puerta.**
	(OO-seh soo YAH-beh pah-rah ah-BREER lah P'WEHR-tah)
card	**tarjeta**
	(tar-HEH-tah)

Ring the bell.	**Toque el timbre.**
	(TOH-keh ehl TEEM-breh)
Sign in.	**Al entrar, escriba su nombre y la hora.**
	(ahl en-TRAHR eh-SKREE-bah soo NOHM-breh ee lah OR-ah)
When you leave . . .	**Cuando salga del trabajo...**
	(kwan-doh SAHL-gah del tra-BAH-hoh)
sign out.	**escriba su nombre y la hora.**
	eh-SKREE-bah soo NOHM-breh ee lah OR-ah)
Go out the back door.	**Salga por la puerta de atrás.**
	(SAHL-gah por lah P'WEHR-tah deh ah-TRAHS)
Lock the door behind you.	**Cierre la puerta con llave.**
	(S'YEHR-reh lah P'WEHR-tah kohn YAH-beh)
Make sure the door is locked.	**Asegúrese de que la puerta esté cerrada.**
	(ah-seh-GOO-reh-seh deh keh lah P'WEHR-tah eh-STEH sehr-RAH-thah)
Do not let anyone in when you leave.	**No deje que nadie entre cuando usted salga.**
	(NOH DEH-heh keh-NAH-th'yeh EN-treh kwahn-doh oo-STED SAL-gah)

Hotel Employees

These phrases will announce the type of staff you are looking for. Keep in mind that when the word for a male employee ends in **o**, the female counterpart will end in **a**; when the word for a male employee ends in **or**, the female counterpart will end in **ora**. Words for a male employee that end in **e**, **ista**, or **I** are the same for a female employee. The word for *dishwasher*, **lavaplatos**, does not change according to number or gender. It is a combination word that means, literally, "dishes washer."

We need <u>cleaning staff</u>.	**Necesitamos <u>personal para limpieza</u>.** (neh-seh-see-TAH-mohs pehr-soh-NAHL pah-rah leemp-YEH-sah)
laundry workers	**lavanderos / lavanderas** (lah-bahn-DEH-rohs / lah-ban-DEH-rahs)
kitchen staff	**personal para la cocina** (pehr-soh-NAHL pah-rah lah koh-SEE-nah)
cooks	**cocineros / cocineras** (koh-see-NEH-rohs / koh-see-NEH-rahs)
dishwashers	**lavaplatos** (lah-bah-PLAH-tohs)
busers	**ayudantes de meseros** (ah-yoo-THAN-tehs deh meh-SEH-rohs)

indoor maintenance specialists	**especialistas en el mantenimiento del interior del hotel**
	(eh-speh-s'yah-LIS-tahs en el mahn-teh-nee-M'YEN-to del een-teh-R'YOR del oh-TELL)

Dress Codes and Policies for Employees

Here are phrases that will help you explain your policies regarding employee uniforms and dress codes. In Spanish-speaking countries, uniforms are used for a wider variety of jobs than here. Uniforms are an accepted part of life, beginning at school age. The word **uniforme** covers not only the clothing one wears at work, but also may include guidelines for hairstyle, the wearing of jewelry, or other restrictions normally included in what is called a "dress code" here.

This is your uniform.	**Este es su uniforme.**
	(EH-steh es soo oo-nee-FOR-meh)
Change into your uniform as soon as you arrive.	**Póngase el uniforme en cuanto llegue al trabajo.**
	(POHNG-gah-seh el oo-nee-FOR-meh en kwahn-toh YEH-geh ahl trah-BAH-ho)
Wear your uniform at all times while at work.	**Lleve su uniforme cuando esté trabajando.**
	(YEH-beh soo oo-nee-FOR-meh kwahn-doh eh-STEH tra-bah-HAHN-doh)

Establishing Policies

Wash your uniform every day.	**Lave su uniforme todos los días.**
	(LAH-beh soo oo-nee-FOR-meh
	TOH-thohs lohs DEE-ahs)
every other day	**un día sí, otro no.**
	(oon DEE-ah SEE oh-troh NOH)
every three days	**cada tres días**
	(KAH-tha TRESS DEE-ahs)
Leave your uniform here.	**Deje su uniforme aquí.**
	(DEH-heh soo oo-nee-FOR-meh
	ah-KEE)
Uniforms will be washed by the	**Los uniformes son lavados por el**
laundry service	**servicio de lavandería.**
	(lohs oo-nee-FOR-mehs sohn
	lah-BAH-thohs por el sehr-BEES-
	yoh deh lah-bahn-deh-REE-ah)
dry-cleaned	**limpiados en seco**
	(leemp-YAH-thohs en SEH-koh)
Wear comfortable shoes.	**Lleve zapatos cómodos.**
	(YEH-beh sah-PAH-tohs
	KOH-moh-thohs)
flat	**bajos**
	(BAH-hohs)
rubber-soled	**con suela de hule**
	(kohn SWEH-lah deh-OO-leh)
tennis shoes	**zapatillas de tenis**
	(sah-pah-TEE-yahs
	deh TEH-neese)
this kind of shoes	**este tipo de zapatos**
	(EH-steh TEE-poh deh
	sah-PAH-tohs)

You (do not) need a hair net.	**(No) debe usar redecilla.**
	([NOH] DEH-beh oo-SAHR reh-deh-SEE-yah)
Please do not wear perfume.	**Por favor, no use perfume.**
	(por fah-BOR NOH OO-seh pehr-FOO-meh)
jewelry	**joyas**
	(HOH-yahs)
rings	**anillos**
	(ah-NEE-yohs)
bracelets	**pulseras**
	(pool-SEH-rahs)
earrings	**aretes**
	(ah-REH-tess)
a necklace	**un collar**
	(oon koh-YAR)
Put your clothes and valuables in your locker.	**Guarde su ropa y sus pertenencias de valor bajo llave.**
	(G'WAHR-deh soo ROH-pah ee soos pehr-teh-NENSE-yahs deh bah-LOHR bah-hoh YAH-beh)
Lock it.	**Ciérrelo con llave.**
	(S'YEHR-reh-loh kohn YAH-beh)
Do not give your locker key to anyone.	**No le dé la llave de su guardarropa a nadie.**
	(NOH leh DEH lah YAH-beh deh soo g'wahr-dahr-ROH-pah ah NAH-th'yeh)
combination	**la clave**
	(lah KLAH-beh)

Equipment and Supplies

In this section, you will find phrases that specify what the hotel provides, and your policies regarding cell phones and the use of equipment.

The hotel will provide all supplies and equipment.	**El hotel proporcionará todos los productos y el equipo que usted necesita para el trabajo.**
	(el oh-TEL proh-por-s'yoh-nah-RAH toh-thohs lohs proh-THOOK-tohs ee el eh-KEE-poh keh oo-STED neh-seh-SEE-tah pah-rah el trah-BAH-hoh)
Do not use equipment until you have had an orientation.	**No use el equipo hasta que haya tenido su sesión de orientación.**
	(NOH OO-seh el eh-KEE-poh ah-stah keh ah-yah teh-nee-thoh soo sess-YOHN deh or-yen-tah-S'YOHN)
Please turn off your cell phone.	**Por favor apague su celular.**
	(por fah-BOR ah-PAH-geh soo seh-loo-LAHR)
Leave your cell phone in your locker.	**Deje su celular en su guardarropa.**
	(DEH-heh soo seh-loo-LAR en soo g'wahr-dah-ROH-pah)
You may check your messages during breaks.	**Usted puede checar sus mensajes durante los descansos.**
	(oo-STED pweh-theh cheh-KAHR soos men-SAH-hehs doo-RAHN-teh lohs dess-KAHN-sohs)

Setting Priorities

These phrases will help you tell your employees what is important to you and to the job. Note that you insert "No" to say that something is *not* necessary or important.

This is (not) <u>necessary</u>.	**Esto (no) es <u>necesario</u>.**
	(EH-stoh [NOH] ess neh-seh-SAHR-yoh)
vital	**imprescindible**
	(eem-press-seen-DEE-bleh)
important	**importante**
	(eem-por-TAHN-teh)
the most important	**lo más importante**
	(loh MAHS eem-por-TAHN-teh)
urgent	**urgente**
	(oor-HEN-teh)

Emergency Policies

Here are phrases that will help you assure your employees that they will be taken care of in case of an emergency.

If you are sick . . .	**Si usted está enfermo/a...**
	(see oo-STED eh-STAH en-FEHR-moh/mah)
do not come to work.	**no venga a trabajar.**
	(NOH BENG-gah ah trah-bah-HAHR)

call the supervisor.

llame al supervisor.

(YAH-meh ahl soo-pehr-

bee-SOR)

If you get hurt . . .

Si usted se lastima...

(see oo-STED seh lah-STEE-mah)

have an accident . . .

tiene un accidente...

(t'yeh-neh oon ahk-see-

THEN-teh)

get sick . . .

se enferma...

(seh en-FEHR-mah)

need assistance . . .

necesita ayuda...

(neh-seh-SEE-tah ah-YOO-thah)

call for the supervisor.

llame al supervisor.

(YAH-meh ahl soo-pehr-

bee-SOR)

the nearest co-worker.

trabajador más cercano.

(trah-bah-hah-THOR MAHS

sehr-KAH-noh)

We will administer first aid.

Le administraremos primeros

auxilios.

(leh ahd-meen-ees-trah-reh-mohs

pree-mehr-ohs ah'ook-SEEL-yohs)

take you home

Lo/La llevaremos a su casa.

(loh/lah yeh-bah-REH-mos ah

soo KAH-sah)

take you to the hospital

Lo/La llevaremos al hospital.

(loh/lah yeh-bah-REH-mos ahl

ohs-pee-TAHL)

We will call a doctor.	**Llamaremos a un médico.**
	(yah-mah-REH-mohs ah oon MEH-thee-koh)
an ambulance	**una ambulancia**
	(oo-nah ahm-boo-LAHN-s'yah)
your family	**a su familia**
	(ah soo fah-MEEL-yah)

Safety Precautions

The Spanish word for *safety* is the same as its word for *security*. Words that end in *ity* in English often have a Spanish counterpart that ends in **dad** or **idad**. Keeping this in mind is a great way to increase your Spanish vocabulary—and remember that these words are always feminine in gender. Just think of the **posibilidades**, for example: **oportunidad, responsabilidad, tranquilidad**.

The following phrases will help you ensure the safety of your employees and others.

safety / security	**la seguridad**
	(lah seh-goo-ree-THAD)
Danger!	**¡Peligro!**
	(peh-LEE-groh)
Be careful!	**¡Tenga cuidado!**
	(TENG-gah kwee-THAH-thoh)
Don't touch that.	**No toque eso.**
	(NOH TOH-keh EH-soh)
It's hot!	**¡Está caliente!**
	(eh-STAH cahl-YEN-teh)
It's heavy.	**Es pesado.**
	(ess peh-SAH-thoh)

Establishing Policies

Get help.	**Busque ayuda.**
	(BOOS-keh ah-YOO-thah)
Do not run.	**No corra**.
	(NOH KOR-rah)
Do not drink alcohol <u>here</u>.	**No tome alcohol <u>aquí</u>.**
	(NOH TOH-meh ahl-koh-OHL ah-KEE)
before coming to work	**antes de venir a trabajar**
	(AHN-tess deh beh-NEER ah
	trah-bah-HAHR)
Do not use drugs.	**No use drogas.**
	(NOH OO-seh DROH-gahs)
Do not smoke inside the hotel.	**No fume dentro del hotel.**
	(NOH FOO-meh den-troh del oh-TELL)
Smoke only during breaks.	**Fume solamente durante los**
	descansos.
	(FOO-meh SOH-lah-men-teh
	doo-rahn-teh lohs
	dess-KAHN-sohs)
Report any suspicious occurrence	**Reporte a su supervisor cualquier**
to the supervisor.	**ocurrencia que le parezca**
	extraña.
	(reh-POR-teh ah soo soo-pehr-bee-
	SOR kwahl-k'yehr oh-koor-RENSE-
	yah keh leh pah-RES-kah
	ek-STRAHN-yah)

Chapter 3

General Instructions

H ere are some handy phrases that you can use for a variety of instructions. Of course, people always appreciate hearing **por favor** and **gracias**. You could also add

Well done!	**¡Bien hecho!**
	(B'YEN EH-choh)
I need the <u>vacuum cleaner</u>.	**Necesito <u>la aspiradora</u>.**
	(neh-seh-SEE-toh lah
	ahs-pee-rah-THOR-ah)
those things	**esas cosas**
	(ESS-ahs KOH-sahs)
Help me.	**Ayúdeme.**
	(ah-YOO-theh-meh)
Help him.	**Ayúdelo.**
	(ah-YOO-theh-loh)
Help them.	**Ayúdelos.**
	(ah-YOO-theh-lohs)
Help us.	**Ayúdenos.**
	(ah-YOO-theh-nos)

Watch me.	**Míreme.**
	(MEE-reh-meh)
Show me.	**Muéstreme.**
	(M'WES-treh-meh)
Tell me.	**Dígame.**
	(DEE-gah-meh)
Give me . . .	**Déme...**
	(DEH-meh)
Do it like this.	**Hágalo así.**
	(AH-gah-loh ah-SEE)
Don't do it like that.	**No lo haga así.**
	(NOH loh AH-gah ah-SEE)
Leave it like that.	**Déjelo así.**
	(DEH-heh-loh ah-SEE)

Remember that you can make many instructions negative by adding "No" at the beginning.

Use this cart.	**Use esta carretilla.**
	(OO-seh ESS-tah kar-reh-TEE-yah)
Don't use that machine.	**No use esa máquina.**
	(NOH OO-seh EH-sah MAH-kee-nah)
this product	**este producto**
	(EH-steh proh-THOOK-toh)
Start.	**Empiece.**
	(em-P'YEH-seh)
Stop.	**Pare.**
	(PAH-reh)
Wait.	**Espere.**
	(eh-SPEH-reh)
Clean up.	**Limpie.**
	(LEEMP-yeh)

General Instructions

Take out the trash.	**Saque la basura.**
	(SAH-keh lah bah-SOO-rah)
Remove that.	**Quite eso.**
	(KEE-teh EH-soh)
<u>Open</u> the door.	**Abra la puerta.**
	(AH-brah lah PWEHR-tah)
close	**cierre**
	(S'YEHR-reh)
Turn on the water.	**Abra la llave del agua.**
	(AH-bra lah YAH-beh del AH-gwah)
Turn off the water.	**Cierre la llave del agua.**
	(S'YEHR-reh lah YAH-beh del AH-gwah)
Turn on the light.	**Encienda la luz.**
	(en-S'YEN-dah lah LOOSE)
Turn off the light.	**Apague la luz.**
	(ah-PAH-geh lah LOOSE)
Lock up.	**Cierre con llave.**
	(S'YEHR-reh kohn YAH-beh)
Don't go <u>there</u>.	**No vaya ahí.**
	(NOH BAH-yah ah-EE)
over there	**allí**
	(ah-YEE)
to that floor	**a ese piso**
	(ah EH-seh PEE-soh)
Don't touch <u>this</u>.	**No toque esto.**
	(NOH TOH-keh ESS-toh)
that	**eso**
	(ESS-oh)
Ask me first.	**Pregúnteme antes.**
	(preh-GOON-teh-meh AHN-tess)

Indicating Order and Repetition of Tasks

When do you want something done? And in what order? Also, you may want something done only once, or perhaps more than once. Use the following expressions to explain your wishes.

Do this <u>first</u>.	**Haga esto <u>primero</u>.**
	(AH-gah EH-stoh pree-MEH-roh)
after that	**luego**
	(L'WEH-goh)
at the same time	**al mismo tiempo**
	(ahl MEEZ-moh T'YEM-poh)
beforehand	**antes**
	(AHN-tess)
afterward	**después**
	(dess-P'WESS)
soon	**pronto**
	(PROHN-toh)
right away	**en seguida**
	(en seh-GHEE-thah)
	ahora mismo
	(ah-OR-ah MEEZ-moh)
now	**ahora**
	(ah-OR-ah)
later	**más tarde**
	(MAHS TAHR-deh)
next week	**la semana próxima**
	(lah seh-MAH-nah PROHK-see-mah)
at the end	**al final**
	(al fee-NAHL)

Do this <u>one time</u>.

Haga esto <u>una vez</u>.

(AH-gah EH-stoh OO-nah BESS)

two times

dos veces

(DOHS BEH-sess)

many times

muchas veces

(MOO-chahs BEH-sess)

Indicating Locations of Things

These expressions will help you tell where things are, or where they should be. Note that certain expressions end with **de**. If the word that follows is of "masculine" gender, like **hotel**, **de** will change to **del**. If the word that follows is of "feminine" gender, like **carretilla**, **de la** is used.

It's <u>here</u>.

Está <u>aquí</u>.

(eh-STAH ah-KEE)

there

allí

(ah-YEE)

in front of the hotel

delante del hotel

(deh-LAHN-teh del oh-TELL)

<u>in front</u> of the cart

<u>delante</u> de la carretilla

(deh-LAHN-teh deh lah

KAHR-reh-TEE-yah)

in back of

detrás de

(deh-TRASS deh)

next to

al lado de

(ahl LAH-thoh deh)

on top of

encima de

(en-SEE-mah deh)

under	**debajo de**
	(de-BAH-hoh deh)
across from / facing	**enfrente de**
	(en-FREN-teh deh)
between the bed and the door	**entre la cama y la puerta**
	(EN-treh lah KAH-mah ee lah P'WEHR-tah)
inside	**adentro**
	(ah-THEN-troh)
outside	**afuera**
	(ah-FWEH-rah)
upstairs (up there)	**arriba**
	(ahr-REE-bah)
downstairs (down there)	**abajo**
	(ah-BAH-hoh)

Going Places and Taking Things

Hotel work involves a lot of moving things from one place to another. These phrases will help you give this kind of instructions. Note that *to the* . . . is **al** before certain words (those that are "masculine" in gender, and **a la** before others (those that are "feminine" in gender). If you learn the entire phrase, you won't have to worry about the gender of the word—it will come naturally.

Come here.	**Venga acá.**
	(BENG-gah ah-KAH)
Bring me the towels.	**Tráigame las toallas.**
	(TRY-gah-meh lahs toh-AH-yahs)
the key	**la llave**
	(lah YAH-beh)

General Instructions

Go . . .	**Vaya...**
	(BAH-yah)
Take this . . .	**Lleve esto...**
	(YEH-beh EH-stoh)
over there.	**para allá.**
	(pah-rah ah-YAH)
to the supervisor.	**al supervisor.**
	(ahl soo-pehr-bee-SOR)
to the lobby.	**al lobby.**
	(ahl LOH-bee)
to the fourth floor.	**al cuarto piso.**
	(al KWAHR-toh PEE-soh)
Put that in the trash.	**Ponga eso en la basura.**
	(POHNG-gah ESS-oh en lah bah-SOO-rah)
in the restaurant	**en el restaurante**
	(en el res-tah'oo-RAHN-teh)
here	**aquí**
	(ah-KEE)
over there	**allí**
	(ah-YEE)

Chapter 4

Specific Tasks for Guest Room Attendants

I n this section, you will find phrases that will explain how you expect your guest rooms to be maintained. The Spanish word for *guest room*—**habitación** (with a silent **h**)—can also refer to any "room" in general. It also means "habitation" in English. Here is another great way to increase your Spanish vocabulary: words that end in *tion*, *sion* and sometimes just *ion* in English often have counterparts in Spanish that end in **ión**. These are always feminine in gender. For your **consideración: sección**, **posición**, **precaución**, **función**.

Do keep in mind that there are some **excepciones**.

the guest room	**la habitación**
	(lah ah-bee-tah-S'YOHN)

Introducing the Guest Rooms

These phrases will help you explain the different types of rooms offered by the hotel.

This is a <u>single room</u>.	**Esta es <u>una habitación individual</u>.**
	(EH-stah es oo-nah ah-bee-tah-
	S'YOHN een-dee-beethe-WAHL)
a double room	**una doble**
	(oo-nah DOH-bleh)
a double with two double beds	**una doble con dos camas de**
	matrimonio
	(oo-nah DOH-bleh kohn DOHS
	KAH-mahs deh
	mah-tree-MOHN-yoh)
a double with one king-size bed	**una doble con una cama**
	extragrande
	(oo-nah DOH-bleh kohn
	oo-nah KAH-mah eks-trah-
	GRAHN-deh)
a suite	**un suite**
	(oon eh-SWEET)
smoking	**fumar**
	(foo-MAHR)
non-smoking	**no fumar**
	(NOH foo-MAHR)

Tasks for Cleaning the Guest Rooms

Here are phrases that specify how you would like your guest rooms to
be cleaned and arranged.

Cleaning the Room and Its Contents

Put the cleaning supplies on
the trolley.

Ponga los limpiadores en el carrito.
(POHNG-gah lohs leemp-yah-THOR-
ess en el kahr-REE-toh)

clean linen

la ropa blanca limpia
(lah ROH-pah BLANG-kah
LEEMP-yah)

Leave the trolley outside the room
you are cleaning.

**Deje el carrito afuera de la
habitación que esté limpiando.**
(DEH-heh el kahr-REE-toh ah-F'WEH-
rah deh lah ah-bee-tah-S'YOHN
keh eh-STEH leemp-YAHN-doh)

Open the curtains.

Abra las cortinas.
(AH-brah lahs kor-TEE-nahs)

Open the windows.

Abra las ventanas.
(AH-brah lahs ben-TAH-nahs)

Remove all trash.

Saque toda la basura.
(SAH-keh TOH-thah lah bah-SOO-rah)

dirty dishes

los platos sucios
(lohs PLAH-tohs SOOS-yohs)

Wash out the trashcans.

Lave los basureros.
(LAH-beh lohs bah-soo-REH-rohs)

Spot-clean the carpet.

Limpie las manchas de la alfombra.
(LEEMP-yeh lahs MAHN-chahs deh
lah ahl-FOHM-brah)

Vacuum the carpet.	**Pase la aspiradora por las alfombras.**
	(PAH-seh lah ah-spee-rah-THOR-ah por lahs ahl-FOHM-brahs)
drapes	**las cortinas gruesas**
	(lahs kor-TEE-nahs gr'WESS-ahs)
baseboards	**los zócalos**
	(lohs SOH-kah-lohs)
Dust the furniture.	**Pase el trapo por los muebles.**
	(PAH-seh el TRAH-poh por lohs M'WEH-blehs)
polish	**lustre**
	(LOO-streh)
Wipe the window sills.	**Limpie las repisas.**
	(LEEMP-yeh lahs reh-PEE-sahs)
blinds	**las persianas**
	(lahs pehr-S'YAH-nahs)
television screen	**la pantalla del televisor**
	(lah pahn-TAH-yah del teh-leh-bee-SOR)
lamps	**las lámparas**
	(lahs LAHM-pah-rahs)
light bulbs	**las bombillas**
	(lahs bohm-BEE-yahs)
Replace any burned out bulbs.	**Cambie las bombillas quemadas.**
	(KAHM-b'yeh lahs bohm-BEE-yahs keh-MAH-thahs)
Do not open the guests' suitcases.	**No abra las maletas de los huéspedes.**
	(NOH AH-brah lahs mah-LEH-tahs deh lohs WESS-peh-thess)

Specific Tasks for Guest Room Attendants

Do not touch the guests' belongings.

No toque las pertenencias de los huéspedes.
(NOH TOH-keh lahs pehr-teh-NENSE-yahs deh lohs WESS-peh-thess)

Do not throw books in the trash.

No tire los libros a la basura.
(NOH TEE-reh lohs LEE-brohs ah lah bah-SOO-rah)

magazines

las revistas
(lahs reh-BEE-stahs)

papers

los papeles
(lohs pah-PELL-ess)

If you are in doubt, don't throw it out.

Si queda una duda, no lo tire.
(see keh-thah oo-nah DOO-thah NOH lo TEE-reh)

If the guest has left a bag for the laundry, send it on.

Si el huésped ha dejado una bolsa para la lavandería, mándesela.
(see el WESS-ped ah deh-HAH-thoh oo-nah BOHL-sah pah-rah lah lah-ban-deh-REE-ah MAHN-deh-seh-lah)

(Do not) hang the guests' clothing.

(No) cuelgue la ropa de los huéspedes.
([NOH] KWELL-geh lah ROH-pah deh lohs WESS-peh-thess)

Fold the guests' clothing.

Doble la ropa de los huéspedes.
(DOH-bleh lah ROH-pah deh lohs WESS-peh-thess)

Leave the guests' clothing at
the foot of the bed.

**Deje la ropa de los huéspedes al
pie de la cama.**

(DEH-heh lah ROH-pah deh lohs
WESS-peh-thess ahl P'YEH deh lah
KAH-mah)

If you find anything of value after
a guest has checked out . . .

**Si encuentra cualquier cosa de
valor después que un huésped
haya salido...**

(see en-KWEN-trah kwahl-K'YEHR
KOH-sah deh bah-LOR dess-PWESS
keh oon WESS-ped ah-yah sah-
LEE-thoh)

Take it to your supervisor.

Llévela a su supervisor.

(YEH-beh-lah ah soo
soo-pehr-bee-SOR)

the office

la oficina

(lah oh-fee-SEE-nah)

Use this product.

Use este producto.

(OO-seh EH-steh proh-THOOK-toh)

these rags

estos trapos

(EH-stohs TRAH-pohs)

this machine

esta máquina

(EH-stah MAH-kee-nah)

If you see insects or other pests . . .

**Si encuentra insectos u otro animal
dañino...**

(see en-KWEN-trah een-SEK-tohs oo
oh-troh ah-nee-MAHL
dahn-YEE-noh)

Use this spray.

Use este espray.

(OO-seh EH-steh eh-SPRY)

Specific Tasks for Guest Room Attendants

Report it to <u>your supervisor</u>
    Infórmele a su supervisor.
    (een-FOR-meh-leh ah soo
        soo-pehr-bee-SOR)

the office
    la oficina
    (lah oh-fee-SEE-nah)

Changing the Beds

Remove all the <u>bedding</u>.
    Saque toda la ropa de cama.
    (SAH-keh TOH-thah lah ROH-pah deh
        KAH-mah)

blankets
    las frazadas
    (lahs frah-SAH-thahs)

sheets
    las sábanas
    (lahs SAH-bah-nahs)

pillowcases
    las fundas
    (lahs FOON-dahs)

mattress pads
    las cubiertas del colchón
    (lahs koob-YEHR-tahs del
        kohl-CHON)

Air out the <u>pillows</u>.
    Airee las almohadas.
    (eye-REH-eh lahs ahl-moh-AH-thahs)

bedspreads
    las cubrecamas
    (lahs koo-breh-KAH-mahs)

(Do not) remove bedspreads.
    (No) saque las cubrecamas.
    ([NOH] SAH-keh lahs
        koo-breh-KAH-mahs)

Make the bed.
    Arregle la cama.
    (ahr-REH-gleh lah KAH-mah)

Put the mattress pad on.

Ponga la cubierta del colchón.

(POHNG-gah lah koob-YEHR-tah del kohl-CHOHN)

the bottom sheet

la sábana de abajo

(lah SAH-bah-nah deh ah-BAH-hoh)

the top sheet

la sábana de encima

(lah SAH-bah-nah deh en-SEE-mah)

the blanket

la frazada

(lah frah-SAH-thah)

the bedspread

la cubrecama

(lah koo-breh-KAH-mah)

Tuck in the corners, like this.

Meta las puntas debajo de la cama, así.

(MEH-tah lahs POON-tahs deh-BAH-hoh deh lah KAH-mah ah-SEE)

Fold the top sheet down, like this.

Doble la sábana de encima, así.

(DOH-bleh lah SAH-bah-nah deh en-SEE-mah ah-SEE)

Put on the pillowcases.

Ponga las fundas.

(POHNG-gah lahs FOON-dahs)

Put the pillows on the bed.

Ponga las almohadas en la cama.

(POHNG-gah lahs ahl-moh-AH-thahs en lah KAH-mah)

(Do not) fold the bedspread over the pillows.

(No) doble la cubrecama sobre las almohadas.

([NOH] DOH-bleh lah koo-breh-KAH-mah soh-breh lahs ahl-moh-AH-thahs)

(Do not) turn the bed down.	**(No) prepare la cama para dormir.**
	([NOH] preh-PAH-reh la KAH-mah pah-rah dohr-MEER)
Send soiled bedding to the laundry.	**Mande la ropa de cama sucia a la lavandería.**
	(MAHN-deh lah ROH-pah deh KAH-mah SOOSE-yah ah lah lah-bahn-deh-REE-ah)

Replenishing Supplies in the Room

Make sure a hotel brochure is on the desk.	**Cheque que un folleto del hotel esté en el escritorio.**
	(CHEH-keh keh oon foh-YEH-toh del oh-TELL eh-STEH en el eh-skree-TOR-yoh)
a pen	**una pluma / un lapicero**
	(oo-nah PLOO-mah / oon lah-pee-SEH-roh)
a notepad	**un cuadernillo para notas**
	(oon kwah-thehr-NEE-yoh pah-rah NOH-tahs)
a room service menu	**un menú para servicio a la habitación**
	(oon meh-NOO pah-rah sehr-BEESE-yoh ah lah ah-bee-tah-S'YOHN)
a bag for the laundry	**una bolsa para la ropa sucia**
	(oo-nah BOHL-sah pah-rah lah roh-pah-SOOSE-yah)

Check the <u>coffee maker</u>.	**Cheque la cafetera.**
	(CHEH-keh lah kah-feh-TEH-rah)
coffee	**el café**
	(el kah-FEH)
tea bags	**el té**
	(el TEH)
sugar	**el azúcar**
	(el ah-SOO-kar)
sugar substitute	**el sustituto del azúcar**
	(el soose-tee-TOO-toh del
	ah-SOO-kar)
creamer	**el sustituto de la crema**
	(el soose-tee-TOO-toh deh lah
	KREH-mah)
cups	**las tazas**
	(lahs TAH-sahs)
spoons	**las cucharas**
	(lahs koo-CHAH-rahs)

Tasks for Cleaning the Bathrooms

Here are some phrases for giving instructions for cleaning the bathrooms.

Remove <u>used towels</u>.	**Saque las toallas usadas.**
	(SAH-keh lahs toh-AH-yahs
	oo-SAH-thahs)
the bathmat	**el tapete del baño**
	(el tah-PEH-teh del BAHN-yoh)
the trash	**la basura**
	(lah bah-SOO-rah)

Specific Tasks for Guest Room Attendants

Wash the trash can.
Lave el basurero.
(LAH-beh el bah-soo-REH-roh)

Clean all surfaces.
Limpie todas las superficies.
(LEEMP-yeh TOH-thahs lahs
soo-pehr-FEESE-yehs)

Clean the shower curtain.
Limpie la cortina de la ducha.
(LEEMP-yeh lah kor-TEE-nah deh lah
DOO-chah)

Scrub the bathtub.
Friegue la bañera.
(FR'YEH-geh lah bahn-YEH-rah)

    soap holders
las jaboneras
(lahs hah-boh-NEH-rahs)

    sink
el lavabo
(el lah BAH-boh)

    toilet
el inodoro
(el een-oh-THOH-roh)

    floor
el suelo
(el SWEH-loh)

Clean the mirror.
Limpie el espejo.
(LEEMP-yeh el eh-SPEH-hoh)

Wipe the shower curtain rail.
**Pásele el trapo por la barra de la
cortina de la ducha.**
(PAH-seh-leh el TRAH-poh por lah
BAHR-rah deh lah kor-TEE-nah
deh lah DOO-chah)

Use this product.
Use este producto.
(OO-seh EH-steh proh-THOOK-toh)

    these rags
estos trapos
(EH-stohs TRAH-pohs)

    a sponge
una esponja
(oo-nah eh-SPOHN-hah)

a wet mop	**un trapeador mojado**
	(oon trah-peh-ah-THOR
	moh-HAH-thoh)
Dry all surfaces.	**Seque todas las superficies.**
	(SEH-keh TOH-thahs lahs
	soo-pehr-FEESE-yehs)
Check the supply of Kleenex.	**Cheque la cantidad de Kleenex.**
	(CHEH-keh lah kahn-tee-THAD deh
	KLEE-neks)
toilet paper	**papel higiénico**
	(pah-PELL ee-H'YEH-nee-koh)
soap	**jabón**
	(hah-BOHN)
shampoo	**champú**
	(chahm-POO)
shower caps	**gorras para la ducha**
	(GOR-rahs pah-rah lah
	DOO-chah)
body lotion	**loción para el cuerpo**
	(loh-S'YOHN pah-rah el
	KWEHR-poh)

Final Tasks

These are the last things to be done to get the room ready for the next guest.

Close the windows.	**Cierre las ventanas.**
	(S'YEHR-reh lahs ben-TAH-nahs)
Close the curtains.	**Cierre las cortinas.**
	(S'YEHR-reh lahs kor-TEE-nahs)

Specific Tasks for Guest Room Attendants

Draw the drapes halfway.

Deje las cortinas gruesas entreabiertas.

(DEH-heh lahs kor-TEE-nahs gr'WESS-ahs ehn-treh-ah-B'YEHR-tahs)

Check the <u>closet</u>.

Cheque <u>la guardarropa</u>.

(CHEH-keh lah gwahr-dahr-ROH-pah)

bureau drawers

los cajones de la cómoda

(lohs kah-HOH-ness deh lah KOH-moh-thah)

Turn on the air conditioner.

Encienda el acondicionador de aire.

(en-S'YEN-dah el ah-kohn-dees-s'yon-ah-thor deh EYE-reh)

Set the <u>air conditioning</u> at <u>medium</u>.

Ponga <u>el aire acondicionado</u> a una temperatura <u>moderada</u>.

(POHNG-gah el EYE-reh ah-kohn-deese-yoh-NAH-thoh ah oo-nah tem-peh-rah-TOO-rah moh-theh-RAH-thah)

heating unit

la calefacción

(lah kah-lee-fahk-S'YOHN)

high

alta

(AHL-tah)

low

baja

(BAH-hah)

Turn off the air-conditioner.

Apague el acondicionador de aire.

(ah-PAH-geh el ah-kohn-dees-s'yon-ah-thor deh EYE-reh)

Place fresh fruit in the basket.

Coloque frutas en la cesta.

(koh-LOH-keh FROO-tahs en lah SEH-stah)

Place chocolates on the pillow.	**Ponga chocolates sobre la almohada.**
	(POHNG-gah choh-koh-lah-tess soh-breh lah ahl-moh-AH-thah)
Hang the "Do not Disturb" sign on the inside doorknob.	**Cuelgue el letrero de "No estorbar" en la perilla interior de la puerta.**
	(KWELL-geh el leh-TREH-roh deh no ehs-tor-BAHR en lah peh-REE-yah een-tehr-YOR deh lah PWEHR-tah)

Interacting with Guests

Here you will find phrases for explaining your policies regarding the interaction of the cleaning staff with guests. The Spanish word for *guest* is the same for a male or female, but **el** or **la** indicate whether the guest is a male or female:

the guest (male)	**el huésped**
	(el WESS-ped)
the guest (female)	**la huésped**
	(lah WESS-ped)
the guests (all male or mixed group)	**los huéspedes**
	(lohs WESS-peh-thess)
the guests (female)	**las huéspedes**
	(lahs WESS-peh-thess)
Be courteous to the guests at all times.	**Siempre trate a los huéspedes con cortesía.**
	(S'YEM-preh TRAH-teh ah lohs WESS-peh-thess kohn kor-teh-SEE-ah)

Specific Tasks for Guest Room Attendants

Knock before entering a room.

Toque a la puerta antes de entrar en una habitación.

(TOH-keh ah lah P'WEHR-tah ahn-tess deh en-TRAR en oo-nah ah-bee-tah-S'YOHN)

Leave the door open when in the room with a guest.

Deje abierta la puerta cuando esté en la habitación con un huésped.

(DEH-heh ah-b'YEHR-tah lah P'WEHR-tah kwahn-doh eh-STEH en lah ah-bee-tah-S'YOHN kohn oon WESS-ped)

If a guest is in the room when you enter . . .

Si un huésped está en la habitación cuando usted entre...

(see oon WESS-ped eh-STAH en lah ah-bee-tah-S'YOHN kwahn-doh oo-STED en-treh)

say "I'm sorry" and leave immediately.

diga "I'm sorry" y salga inmediatamente.

(DEE-gah "I'm sorry" ee SAHL-gah een-meh-TH'YAH-tah-men-teh)

If the guest does not leave before 11 A.M. . . . .

Si el huésped no sale antes de las once de la mañana...

(see el WESS-ped noh-SAH-leh ahn-tess deh lahs OHN-seh deh lah mahn-YAH-nah) ask your supervisor for instructions.

pídale instrucciones a su supervisor.

(PEE-thah-leh een-strook-S'YOH-ness ah soo soo-pehr-bee-SOR)

do not clean the room.

no limpie la habitación.

(NOH LEEMP-yeh lah ah-bee-tah-S'YOHN)

clean the room in the afternoon.

limpie la habitación en la tarde.

(LEEMP-yeh lah ah-bee-tah-S'YOHN en lah TAR-deh)

Chapter 5

Specific Tasks for the Laundry Unit

The word for *laundry room* in Spanish is literally, "a place for washing." It's also the name of the place where laundry can be done comercially.

the laundry room

la lavandería
(lah lah-bahn-deh-REE-ah)

Introducing the Work in the Laundry

These phrases will explain the kind of work done in the hotel laundry unit.

This job requires . . .

Este trabajo requiere...
(eh-steh trah-BAH-hoh
reh-K'YEH-reh)

lifting heavy loads.

que levante cargas pesadas.
(keh leh-BAHN-teh KAHR-gahs
peh-SAH-thahs)

lifting as much as 75 pounds	**que levante hasta 75 libras** (keh leh-BAHN-teh ah-stah seh-TEN-tah ee SEENG-koh LEE-brahs)
pushing heavy carts	**que empuje carritos pesados** (keh em-POO-heh kahr-REE-tohs peh-SAH-thohs)
pulling carts that weigh up to 400 pounds	**que jale carritos que pesen hasta 400 libras** (keh HAH-leh kah-REE-tohs keh peh-sen ah-stah kwah-troh-S'YEN-tas LEE-brahs)
withstanding high temperatures	**que aguante temperaturas altas** (keh ah-GWAHN-teh tem-peh-rah-TOO-rahs AHL-tahs)
bending	**que se agache** (keh seh ah-GAH-cheh)
kneeling	**que se arrodille** (keh seh ahr-roh-THEE-yeh)
sorting laundry	**que separe la ropa sucia** (keh seh-PAH-reh lah roh-pah SOOSE-yah)
marking	**que marque la ropa** (keh MAR-keh la roh-pah)
folding	**doble** (DOH-bleh)
wrapping	**envuelva** (en-B'WELL-bah)
packing	**empaque** (em-PAH-keh)

distributing	**distribuya**
	(dee-stree-BOO-yah)
weighing	**pese**
	(PEH-seh)
recording	**anote**
	(ah-NOH-teh)
using large machines	**que use máquinas**
	industriales
	(keh OO-seh MAH-kee-nahs
	een-doos-TR'YAH-less)

Operating Laundry Machines

Here are instructions for using different machines in the laundry unit. You could refer to any one of them as:

the machine	**la máquina**
	(lah MAH-kee-nah)

The Washing Machines

washing machine	**la máquina de lavar**
	(lah MAH-kee-nah deh lah-BAHR)
Separate the laundry by category.	**Separe la ropa sucia por categoría.**
	(seh-PAH-reh lah roh-pah SOOSE-yah
	por kah-teh-goh-REE-ah)
Put the bedding in this /	**Ponga la ropa de cama en esta /**
that basket.	**esa canasta.**
	(POHNG-gah lah ROH-pah deh
	KAH-mah en EH-stah / EH-sah
	kah-NAH-stah)

73

sheets	**las sábanas**
	(lahs SAH-bah-nahs)
pillow cases	**las fundas**
	(lahs FOON-dahs)
blankets	**las frazadas**
	(lahs frah-SAH-thahs)
towels	**las toallas**
	(lahs toh-AH-yahs)
table linen	**la mantelería**
	(lah mahn-teh-leh-REE-ah)
tablecloths	**los manteles**
	(lohs mahn-TEH-less)
napkins	**las servilletas**
	(lahs sehr-bee-YEH-tahs)
uniforms	**los uniformes**
	(lohs oo-nee-FOR-mess)
individual guest's personal laundry	**la ropa personal de los huéspedes**
	(lah ROH-pah pehr-soh-NAHL deh lohs WESS-peh-thess)
Inspect linen for <u>stains</u>.	**Cheque si hay <u>manchas</u> en la ropa blanca.**
	(CHEH-keh see eye MAHN-chahs en lah ROH-pah BLAHNG-kah)
tears	**roturas**
	(roh-TOO-rahs)
holes	**agujeros**
	(ah-goo-HEH-rohs)

Specific Tasks for the Laundry Unit

Treat blood stains with cold water.

Use agua fría para quitar las manchas de sangre.

(OO-seh AH-gwah FREE-ah pah-rah kee-TAHR lahs MAHN-chahs deh SAHNG-greh)

Spray stains with this product.

Use este producto para quitar manchas.

(OO-seh EH-steh proh-THOOK-toh pah-rah kee-TAHR MAHN-chahs)

Fill the machine with dirty sheets to this level.

Llene la máquina hasta aquí con sábanas sucias.

(YEH-neh lah MAH-kee-nah AH-stah ah-KEE kohn SAH-bah-nahs SOOSE-yahs)

Use hot water.

Use agua caliente.

(OO-seh AH-gwah kahl-YEN-teh)

cold water

agua fría

(AH-gwah FREE-ah)

Turn on the hot water.

Abra la llave del agua caliente.

(AH-brah lah YAH-beh del AH-gwah kahl-YEN-teh)

Measure and add detergent.

Mida y agregue detergente.

(MEE-thah ee ah-GREH-geh deh-tehr-HEN-teh)

bleach

lejía

(leh-HEE-ah)

fabric softener

suavizante de telas

(swah-bee-SAHN-teh deh TEH-lahs)

this product

este producto

(EH-steh proh-THOOK-toh)

Set the cycle.	**Seleccione el programa de lavado**.
	(seh-lek-S'YOH-neh el proh-GRAH-mah deh lah-BAH-thoh)
Set the size of the load.	**Seleccione el tamaño de la tanda.**
	(seh-lek-S'YOH-neh el tah-MAHN-yoh deh lah TAHN-dah)
Set the timer.	**Ponga el reloj.**
	(POHNG-gah el reh-LOH)
Close the <u>door</u>.	**Cierre <u>la puerta</u>.**
	(S'YEHR-reh lah P'WEHR-tah)
lid	**la tapa**
	(lah TAH-pah)
Push the dial in.	**Empuje el indicador para dentro**.
	(em-POO-heh el een-dee-kah-THOR pah-rah THEN-troh)
Turn the dial to the right.	**Gire el indicador a la derecha.**
	(HEE-reh el een-dee-kah-THOR ah lah deh-REH-chah)
Go to "start."	**Pare donde indica "start".**
	(PAH-reh dohn-deh een-DEE-kah "START")
Pull the dial out.	**Jale el indicador.**
	(HAH-leh el een-dee-kah-THOR)
The machine will start.	**La máquina se pondrá en marcha**.
	(lah MAH-kee-nah seh pohn-DRAH en MAR-chah)
When the machine is running . . .	**Cuando la máquina esté en marcha...**
	(kwahn-doh lah MAH-kee-nah eh-STEH en MAHR-chah)

Specific Tasks for the Laundry Unit

the machine will be very hot.	**la máquina estará caliente.**
	(lah MAH-kee-nah eh-stah-RAH kahl-YEN-teh)
do not touch the machine.	**no toque la máquina.**
	(NOH TOH-keh lah MAH-kee-nah)
do not open the machine door.	**no abra la puerta de la máquina.**
	(NOH AH-brah lah PWEHR-tah deh lah MAH-kee-nah)
When the cycle is completed . . .	**Cuando el programa se haya terminado...**
	(kwahn-doh el proh-GRAH-ma seh ah-yah tehr-mee-NAH-thoh)
remove the items from the machine.	**saque los artículos de la máquina.**
	(SAH-keh lohs ahr-TEE-koo-lohs deh lah MAH-kee-nah)
put the items in a basket.	**ponga los artículos en una canasta.**
	(POHNG-gah lohs ahr-TEE-koo-lohs en oo-nah kah-NAH-stah)
transfer the articles to a dryer.	**pase los artículos a una secadora.**
	(PAH-seh lohs ahr-TEE-koo-lohs ah oo-nah seh-kah-THOR-ah)

The Dryers

Load the wet articles into the dryer.
Ponga los artículos mojados en la secadora.
(POHNG-gah lohs ahr-TEE-koo-lohs moh-HAH-thohs en lah seh-kah-THOR-ah)

Set the temperature.
Seleccione la temperatura deseada.
(seh-lek-S'YOH-neh lah tem-peh-rah-TOO-rah deh-seh-AH-thah)

Set the timer.
Ponga el reloj.
(POHNG-gah el reh-LOH)

Push the button to start the machine.
Apriete el botón para encender la máquina.
(ah-PR'YEH-teh el boh-TOHN pah-rah en-sen-DEHR lah MAH-kee-nah)

When the cycle ends . . .
Cuando se termine el programa...
(kwahn-doh seh tehr-MEE-neh el proh-GRAH-mah)

remove all the items.
saque todos los artículos.
(SAH-keh TOH-thohs lohs ahr-TEE-koo-lohs)

place the items in a basket.
ponga los artículos en una canasta.
(POHNG-gah lohs ahr-TEE-koo-lohs en oo-nah kah-NAH-stah)

Specific Tasks for the Laundry Unit

Put the basket on the conveyor belt.	**Ponga la canasta en la cinta transportadora.**
	(POHNG-gah lah kah-NAH-stah en lah SEEN-tah trans-por-tah-THOR-ah)
Take the items to a <u>linen presser</u>.	**Lleve los artículos a una <u>planchadora</u>.**
	(YEH-beh lohs ahr-TEE-koo-lohs ah oo-nah plahn-chah-THOR-ah)
table linen ironer	**planchadora de mantelería**
	(plahn-chah-THOR-ah deh mahn-teh-leh-REE-ah)
<u>towel</u> folder	**dobladora de <u>toallas</u>**
	(doh-blah-THOR-ah deh toh-AH-yahs)
sheet	**sábanas**
	(SAH-bah-nahs)
blanket	**frazadas**
	(frah-SAH-thahs)
napkin	**servilletas**
	(sehr-bee-YEH-tahs)

The Pressing and Folding Machines

Be careful.	**Tenga mucho cuidado.**
	(TENG-gah MOO-choh kwee-THAH-thoh)
The machines are very hot.	**Las máquinas están muy calientes.**
	(lahs MAH-kee-nahs eh-STAHN M'WEE kahl-YEN-tess)

Do not touch the machines.	**No toque las máquinas.**
	(NOH TOH-keh lahs MAH-kee-nahs)
Adjust the machine to your height.	**Ajuste la máquina a su altura.**
	(ah-HOO-steh lah MAH-kee-nah ah
	soo ahl-TOO-rah)
To operate the linen feeder . . .	**Para operar el alimentador...**
	(pah-rah oh-peh-RAHR el
	ah-lee-men-tah-THOR)

    <u>loosen</u> the fabric, like this.   **suelte la tela, así.**
        (SWELL-teh lah TEH-lah ah-SEE)

    untangle   **desenrede**
        (dess-en-REH-theh)

    grab   **agarre**
        (ah-GAHR-reh)

    feed   **introduzca**
        (een-troh-DOOSE-kah)

    <u>fin</u>d a corner   **busque una punta del artículo**
        (BOOSE-keh oo-nah POON-tah
        del ar-TEE-koo-loh)

    mark   **marque**
        (MAHR-keh)

    feed the corner into the   **introduzca la punta en la**
    machine   **máquina**
        (een-troh-DOOSE-kah lah
        POON-tah en lah
        MAH-kee-nah)

    feed the articles into the ironers   **introduzca los artículos en**
        las planchadoras
        (een-troh-DOOSE-kah lohs
        ahr-TEE-koo-lohs en lahs
        plahn-chah-THOR-ahs)

Specific Tasks for the Laundry Unit

<u>evenly space</u> the articles on the feeder ribbon

espacie los artículos uniformemente en la cinta de alimentación

(eh-SPAHS-yeh lohs ahr-TEE-koo-lohs oo-nee-for-meh-MEN-teh en lah SEEN-tah deh ah-lee-men-tah-S'YOHN)

guide

guíe

(GHEE-eh)

smooth wrinkles

alise las arrugas

(ah-LEE-seh lahs ahr-ROO-gahs)

If the machine jams . . .

Si la máquina se tranca...

(see lah MAH-kee-nah seh TRAHNG-kah)

push this button.

apriete este botón.

(ah-PR'YEH-teh eh-steh boh-TOHN)

remove the jammed piece.

saque el artículo atascado.

(SAH-keh el ahr-TEE-koo-loh ah-tahs-KAH-thoh)

re-insert the piece into machine.

meta el artículo en la máquina de nuevo.

(MEH-tah el ar-TEE-koo-loh en lah MAH-kee-nah deh N'WEH-boh)

Stacking and Packing Finished Items

These phrases will help you explain to your staff what they should do with the laundry after it is washed, dried, ironed, and folded.

Stack the folded items, like this.	**Apile los artículos doblados, así.**
	(ah-PEE-leh lohs ahr-TEE-koo-lohs doh-BLAH-thohs ah-SEE)
Wrap the guests' clothing.	**Envuelva la ropa de los huéspedes.**
	(en-B'WELL-bah lah ROH-pah deh lohs WESS-peh-thess)
Hang it.	**Cuélguela.**
	(KWELL-geh-lah)
Place it in a plastic bag.	**Colóquela en una bolsa de plástico.**
	(koh-LOH-keh-lah en oo-nah BOHL-sah deh PLAH-stee-koh)
Send it to the distributor.	**Mándela al destribuidor.**
	(MAHN-deh-lah ahl dee-stree-b'wee-THOR)
Place it on the cart.	**Póngala en el carrito**.
	(POHNG-gah-lah en el kar-REE-toh)

Laundry Room Maintenance

Some of your workers will be asked to keep the laundry room in working order. These phrases will help you explain the details.

Monitor the supplies.	**Cheque la cantidad de productos que se usan.**
	(CHEH-keh lah kahn-tee-THAD deh proh-THOOK-tohs keh seh O-sahn)

Specific Tasks for the Laundry Unit

Order the supplies, as necessary.

Ordene los productos cuando sea necesario.

(or-theh-neh lohs proh-THOOK-tohs kwahn-doh seh-ah neh-seh-SAHR-yoh)

Clean <u>the machine</u>, like this.

Limpie <u>la máquina</u>, así.

(LEEMP-yeh lah MAH-kee-nah ah-SEE)

    the lint filters

        los filtros

        (lohs FEEL-trohs)

    these parts of the machine

        estas partes de la máquina

        (EH-stahs PAR-tehs deh lah MAH-kee-nah)

Replace the filter bags.

Cambie las bolsas del filtro.

(KAHM-b'yeh lahs BOHL-sahs del FEEL-troh)

Report to your supervisor <u>needed repairs</u>.

Informe a su supervisor sobre <u>reparaciones necesarias</u>.

(een-FOR-meh ah soo soo-pehr-bee-SOR soh-breh reh-pah-rah-S'YOH-ness neh-seh-SAHR-yahs)

    unsafe conditions

        condiciones peligrosas

        (kohn-dee-S'YOH-ness peh-lee-GROH-sahs)

    damaged linen

        ropa blanca dañada

        (roh-pah BLAHNG-kah dahn-YAH-thah)

Chapter 6

Specific Instructions for Kitchen and Food Service Staff

I n this section, you will find phrases for explaining to your employees how your kitchen and restaurant service works.

Working in the Kitchen

These phrases will help you introduce the kitchen and kitchen chores to your employees.

In Spanish, the words that refer to cooking are very similar:

to cook	**cocinar**
	(koh-see-NAHR)
the cook	**el cocinero / la cocinera**
	(el koh-see-NEH-roh /
	lah koh-see-NEH-rah)
the cuisine	**la cocina**
	(lah koh-SEE-nah)
the kitchen	**la cocina**
	(lah koh-SEE-nah)

Consider this tongue-twister:

The cook cooks Chinese food in the kitchen.	**La cocinera cocina cocina china en la cocina.**

Getting Ready to Work

The word for *boss* in Spanish is the same as the word for *chef*:

the boss / the chef	**el jefe / la jefa**
	(el HEH-feh / lah HEH-fah)
The chef could also be called:	**el cocinero / la cocinera principal**
	(el koh-see-NEH-roh / lah koh-see-NEH-rah preen-see-PAHL)
The chef is in charge of the kitchen.	**El cocinero principal es el jefe de la cocina.**
	(el koh-see-NEH-roh preen-see-PAHL es el HEH-feh deh lah koh-SEE-nah)
Follow all instructions given by <u>the chef</u>.	**Siga las instrucciones <u>del jefe</u>.**
	(SEE-gah lahs een-strook-SYOH-ness del HEH-feh)
your supervisor	**de su supervisor**
	(deh soo soo-pehr-bee-SOR)
Wash your hands <u>as soon as</u> you enter the kitchen.	**Lávese las manos <u>en cuanto</u> entre en la cocina.**
	(LAH-beh-seh lahs MAH-nohs en kwahn-toh en-treh en lah koh-SEE-nah)
every time	**cada vez que**
	(KAH-thah BESS keh)

after handling raw meat or meat products	**después de tocar la carne cruda o los productos cárnicos** (dess-PWESS deh toh-KAHR lah KAHR-neh KROO-thah oh lohs proh-THOOK-tohs KAHR-nee-kohs)
before preparing <u>salads</u>	**antes de preparar <u>las ensaladas</u>** (ahn-tess deh preh-pah-RAHR lahs en-sah-LAH-thahs)
fruit	**las frutas** (lahs FROO-tahs)
Wear <u>a hairnet</u>.	**Lleve <u>una redecilla</u>.** (YEH-beh oo-nah reh-theh-SEE-yah)
a cap	**una gorra** (oo-nah GOR-rah)
plastic gloves	**guantes de plástico** (GWAHN-tess deh PLAH-stee-koh)
a uniform	**un uniforme** (oon oo-nee-FOR-meh)
an apron	**un delantal** (oon deh-lahn-TAHL)

Preparing Food

Wash this / these.	**Lave esto / estos.** (LAH-beh EH-stoh / EH-stohs)

Peel the fruit.	**Pele la fruta.**
	(PEH-leh lah FROO-tah)
vegetables	**los vegetales**
	(lohs beh-heh-TAH-less)
shrimp	**los camarones**
	(lohs kah-mah-ROH-ness)
Cut it in thick slices.	**Córtelo en rodajas gruesas.**
	(KOR-teh-loh en roh-THAH-hahs GR'WESS-ahs)
thin	**finas**
	(FEE-nahs)
Chop this in large chunks	**Corte esto en trozos grandes.**
	(KOR-teh EH-stoh en troh-sohs GRAHN-dess)
this size	**de este tamaño**
	(deh EH-steh tah-MAHN-yoh)
small	**pequeños**
	(peh-KEN-yohs)
fine	**finos**
	(FEE-nohs)
Remove this part.	**Saque esta parte.**
	(SAH-keh EH-stah PAHR-teh)
Leave that part.	**Deje esa parte.**
	(DEH-heh EH-sah PAHR-teh)
Marinate it.	**Déjelo en adobo.**
	(DEH-heh-loh en ah-THOH-boh)
Refrigerate it for twenty-four hours.	**Déjelo en el refrigerador por veinticuatro horas.**
	(DEH-heh-loh en el reh-free-heh-rah-THOR por bayn-tee-KWAH-troh OH-rahs)

Put it in the freezer.	**Póngalo en el congelador.**
	(POHNG-gah-loh en el kohn-heh-lah-THOR)
Take it out of the <u>freezer</u>.	**Sáquelo <u>del congelador</u>.**
	(SAH-keh-loh del kohn-heh-lah-THOR)
refrigerator	**del refrigerador**
	(del reh-free-heh-rah-THOR)
Let it <u>defrost</u>.	**Deje <u>que se descongele</u>.**
	(DEH-heh keh seh dess-kohn-HEH-leh)
cool	**que se enfríe**
	(keh seh en-FREE-eh)

Utensils for Preparing Food

Use <u>this knife</u>.	**Use <u>este cuchillo</u>.**
	(OO-seh eh-steh koo-CHEE-yoh)
this fork	**este tenedor**
	(eh-steh teh-neh-THOR)
this spoon	**esta cuchara**
	(eh-stah koo-CHAH-rah)
this bowl	**este tazón**
	(eh-steh tah-SOHN)
this utensil	**este utensilio**
	(eh-steh oo-ten-SEEL-yoh)
the grater	**el rallador**
	(el rah-yah-THOR)
the peeler	**el pelapapas**
	(el peh-lah-PAH-pahs)
the mixer	**la batidora**
	(lah bah-tee-THOR-ah)

the blender	**el batidor**
	(el bah-tee-THOR)
a chopper	**una picadora**
	(oo-nah pee-kah-THOR-ah)
a bread slicer	**una máquina rebanadora**
	(oo-nah MAH-kee-nah
	reh-bah-nah-THOR-ah)
a meat slicer	**una máquina de cortar**
	fiambre
	(oo-nah MAH-kee-nah deh
	kor-tahr F'YAM-breh)
a colander	**un colador**
	(oon koh-lah-THOR)
a strainer	**un escurridor**
	(oon eh-skoo-ree-THOR)
a sifter	**un tamiz**
	(oon tah-MEESE)
a rolling pin	**un rodillo**
	(oon roh-THEE-yoh)

Cooking

Put the pot on the stove.	**Ponga la olla en la estufa.**
	(POHNG-gah lah OH-yah en lah
	eh-STOO-fah)
in the oven	**en el horno**
	(en el OR-noh)
at low heat	**a una temperatura baja**
	(ah oo-nah tem-peh-rah-too-
	rah BAH-hah)

Specific Instructions for Kitchen and Food Service Staff

lower   **más baja**
(MAHS BAH-hah)

medium   **medio alta**
(MEH-th'yoh AHL-tah)

high   **alta**
(AHL-tah)

higher   **más alta**
(MAHS AHL-tah)

Add a little oil   **Añada un poco de aceite.**
(ahn-YAH-thah oon poh-koh deh
ah-SAY-teh)

less   **menos**
(MEH-nohs)

more   **más**
(MAHS)

these ingredients   **estos ingredientes**
(EH-stohs een-greh-TH'YEN-
tess)

the butter   **la mantequilla**
(lah mahn-teh-KEE-yah)

the vegetables   **los vegetales**
(los beh-heh-TAH-less)

the meat   **la carne**
(lah KAHR-neh)

the fish   **el pescado**
(el pess-KAH-thoh)

the breadcrumbs   **las migas de pan**
(lahs MEE-gahs deh PAHN)

the milk   **la leche**
(lah LEH-cheh)

the eggs	**los huevos**
	(lohs WEH-bohs)
the oil	**el aceite**
	(el ah-SAY-teh)
the vinegar	**el vinagre**
	(el bee-NAH-greh)
these herbs	**estas hierbas**
	(eh-stahs YEHR-bahs)
this spice	**esta especia**
	(eh-stah eh-SPESS-yah)
this seasoning	**este condimento**
	(eh-steh kohn-dee-MEN-toh)
salt and pepper	**sal y pimienta**
	(SAHL ee peem-YEN-tah)
Cook it for twenty minutes.	**Cocínelo por veinte minutos.**
	(koh-SEE-neh-loh por BAYN-teh mee-NOO-tohs)
Stir it constantly.	**Remuévalo constantemente.**
	(reh-M'WEH-bah-loh kohn-stahn-teh-MEN-teh)
occasionally	**de vez en cuando**
	(de BESS en KWAHN-doh)
Put it in the oven.	**Póngalo en el horno.**
	(POHNG-gah-loh en el OR-noh)
in the toaster	**en el tostador**
	(en el toh-stah-THOR)
on the stove	**en la estufa**
	(en lah eh-STOO-fah)
Take it out of the oven.	**Sáquelo del horno.**
	(SAH-keh-loh del OR-noh)

off the stove	**de la estufa**
	(deh lah eh-STOO-fah)
Bake it for forty minutes.	**Cocínelo en el horno por cuarenta minutos.**
	(koh-SEE-neh-loh en el OR-noh por kwah-REN-tah mee-NOO-tohs)
Roast it at 350 degrees F.	**Cocínelo en el horno a 350 grados F.**
	(koh-SEE-neh-loh en el OR-noh ah tress-YEN-tohs seeng-KWEN-tah grah-thohs EH-feh)
Broil it.	**Áselo a la parrilla.**
	(AH-seh-loh ah lah pahr-REE-yah)
Boil it.	**Hiérvalo.**
	(YEHR-bah-loh)
Braise it.	**Estófelo.**
	(eh-STOH-feh-loh)
Fry it.	**Fríalo.**
	(FREE-ah-loh)

Baking

Break the eggs into a bowl.	**Rompa los huevos en un tazón.**
	(ROHM-pah lohs WEH-bohs en oon tah-SOHN)
Separate the eggs.	**Separe los huevos.**
	(seh-PAH-reh lohs WEH-bohs)
Beat the eggs.	**Bata los huevos.**
	(BAH-tah lohs WEH-bohs)
egg yolks	**las yemas**
	(lahs YEH-mahs)

egg whites	**las claras**
	(lahs KLAH-rahs)
cream	**la crema**
	(lah KREH-mah)
Mix the ingredients.	**Mezcle los ingredientes.**
	(MESS-kleh lohs een-greth-YEN-tes)
Make a cake.	**Haga un pastel.**
	(AH-gah oon pah-STEL)
cookies	**galletas**
	(gah-YEH-tahs)
Cream the butter and sugar.	**Mezcle bien la mantequilla y el azúcar.**
	(MESS-kleh B'YEN lah mahn-teh-KEE-yah ee el ah-SOO-kahr)
Sift the flour.	**Tamice la harina.**
	(tah-MEE-seh lah ah-REE-nah)
Add flour.	**Añada harina.**
	(ahn-YAH-thah ah-REE-nah)
eggs	**huevos**
	(WEH-bohs)
liquids	**líquidos**
	(LEE-kee-thohs)
the other ingredients	**los otros ingredientes**
	(lohs oh-trohs een greth-YEN-tess)
Butter the baking pans, like this.	**Unte los moldes con mantequilla, así.**
	(OON-teh lohs MOHL-dess kohn mahn-teh-KEE-yah ah-SEE)

Pour the batter into the pans.

Vierta la masa a los moldes.

(B'YEHR-tah lah MAH-sah ah lohs
MOHL-dess)

Make the dough.

Haga la masa.

(AH-gah lah MAH-sah)

Roll out the dough.

Estire la masa.

(eh-STEE-reh lah MAH-sah)

Let it sit for thirty minutes.

Déjela por treinta minutos.

(DEH-heh-lah por TRAYN-tah
mee-NOO-tohs)

Arranging Food on Plates and Garnishing

Place the prepared food on
a platter.

**Coloque la comida preparada en
una fuente.**

(koh-LOH-keh lah koh-MEE-thah
preh-pah-rah-thah en oo-nah
FWEN-teh)

individual plates

platos individuales

(PLAH-tohs een-dee-beethe-
WAH-less)

Measure the servings.

Mida las porciones.

(MEE-thah lahs por-S'YOH-ness)

Do it like this.

Hágalo así.

(AH-gah-loh ah-SEE)

Garnish with this.

Decore con esta guarnición.

(deh-KOH-reh kohn eh-stah
wahr-nee-S'YOHN)

parsley

perejil

(peh-reh-HEEL)

mint leaves	**hojas de menta**
	(OH-hahs deh MEN-tah)
lemon wedges	**trozos de limón**
	(troh-sohs deh lee-MOHN)

Emergencies

If . . .	**Si...**
	(SEE)
you cut your finger	**se corta el dedo**
	(seh KOR-tah el DEH-thoh)
burn yourself	**se quema**
	(seh KEH-mah)
slip and fall	**se resbala y se cae**
	(seh res-BAH-lah ee seh KAH-eh)
have an accident	**tiene un accidente**
	(T'YEH-neh oon ahk-see-THEN-teh)
spill something	**derrama algo**
	(dehr-RAH-mah AHL-goh)
break something	**se le rompe algo**
	(seh leh ROHM-peh AHL-goh)
report it to your supervisor.	**informe a su supervisor de lo sucedido.**
	(een-FOR-meh ah soo soo-pehr-bee-SOR deh loh soo-seh-THEE-thoh)
get help right away.	**pida ayuda en seguida.**
	(PEE-thah ah-YOO-thah en seh-GHEE-thah)

clean up right away.	**límpielo en seguida.**
	(LEEMP-yeh-loh en seh-GHEE-thah)
place a sign if the floor is wet.	**coloque un letrero si el suelo está mojado.**
	(koh-LOH keh oon leh-TREH-roh see el SWEH-loh eh-stah moh-HAH-thoh)
If you . . .	**Si usted...**
	(SEE oo-STED)
see <u>insects</u>	**ve <u>insectos</u>**
	(BEH een-SEK-tohs)
cockroaches	**cucarachas**
	(koo-kah-RAH-chahs)
a mouse	**un ratón**
	(oon rah-TOHN)
a rat	**una rata**
	(oo-nah RAH-tah)
other pests	**otro animal indeseable**
	(OH-troh ah-nee-MAHL een-deh-seh-AH-bleh)
tell your supervisor right away.	**dígaselo a su supervisor en seguida.**
	(DEE-gah-seh-loh ah soo soo-pehr-bee-SOR en seh-GHEE-thah)

Kitchen Maintenance

The following phrases are for indicating how to keep the kitchen clean and functioning efficiently.

Organizing the Kitchen

Organize the work area.

Organice el área de trabajo.
(or-gah-NEE-seh el AH-reh-ah de trah-BAH-hoh)

Put everything in its place.

Ponga las cosas en su lugar.
(POHNG-gah lahs KOH-sahs en soo loo-GAHR)

Monitor the pantry supplies.

Cheque que hay suficientes provisiones en la despensa.
(CHEH-keh keh eye soo-fee-S'YEN-tehs proh-bee-S'YOH-ness en lah dess-PEN-sah)

Sweep the kitchen floor after each meal period.

Barra el suelo de la cocina después de cada comida.
(BAHR-rah el SWEH-loh deh lah koh-SEE nah dess-PWESS deh KAH-thah koh-MEE-thah)

Mop the floor after . . .

Pase el trapeador mojado por el piso después de...
(PAH-seh el trah-peh-ah-THOR moh-HAH-thoh por el PEE-soh dess-pwess deh)

any spill

derramar algo sobre el piso
(dehr-rah-MAHR ahl-goh soh-breh el PEE-soh)

Washing Dishes

Wash the dishes.

Lave los platos.
(LAH-beh lohs PLAH-tohs)

Specific Instructions for Kitchen and Food Service Staff

To operate the dishwasher . . .	**Para operar el lavaplatos...**
	(pah-rah oh peh-RAHR el
	lah-bah-PLAH-tohs)
place the dishes in the machine, like this.	**coloque los platos en la máquina, así.**
	(koh-LOH-keh lohs PLAH-tohs
	en lah MAH-kee-nah
	ah-SEE)
cups	**las tazas**
	(lahs TAH-sahs)
serving dishes	**las fuentes**
	(lahs FWEN-tess)
china	**la vajilla**
	(lah bah-HEE-yah)
silverware	**los cubiertos**
	(lohs koob-YEHR-tohs)
pots and pans	**las ollas y las sartenes**
	(lahs OH-yahs ee lahs
	sahr-TEN-ess)
cooking utensils	**los utensilios**
	(lohs oo-ten-SEEL-yohs)
When the cycle is finished . . .	**Cuando el programa se termine...**
	(kwahn-doh el proh-GRAH-mah seh
	tehr-MEE-neh)
place the clean dishes on the storage rack	**coloque los platos limpios en el estante.**
	(koh-LOH-keh lohs PLAH-tohs
	LEEMP-yohs en el
	eh-STAHN-teh)

Wipe the machine clean.

Limpie la máquina con un trapo.
(LEEMP-yeh lah MAH-kee-nah kohn oon TRAH-poh)

Clean the machine.

Limpie la máquina.
(LEEMP-yeh lah MAH-kee-nah)

Monitor the chemical supples.

Fíjese en la cantidad de productos químicos disponibles.
(FEE-heh-seh en lah kahn-tee-THAD deh proh-THOOK-tohs KEE-mee-kohs dees-poh-NEE-bless)

the water temperature of the dishwasher

la temperatura del agua del lavaplatos
(lah tem-peh-rah-too-rah del AH-gwah del lah-bah-PLAH-tohs)

Disposing of Garbage

Put all garbage here.

Ponga los restos de la comida aquí.
(POHNG-gah lohs REH-stohs deh lah koh-MEE-thah ah-KEE)

grease

la grasa
(lah GRAH-sah)

chemicals

los productos químicos
(lohs proh-THOOK-tohs KEE-mee-kohs)

trash

la basura
(lah bah-SOO-rah)

Specific Instructions for Kitchen and Food Service Staff

Put it in this <u>bin</u>.

Póngala en <u>este basurero</u>.

(POHNG-gah-lah en EH-steh
bah-soo-REH-roh)

bag

esta bolsa

(EH-stah BOHL-sah)

Close the garbage bags with plastic ties.

Cierre las bolsas con cierres de plástico.

(S'YEHR-reh lahs BOHL-sahs kohn
S'YEHR-ress deh PLAH-stee-koh)

Clean the trash cans.

Limpie los basureros.

(LEEMP-yeh lohs bah-soo-REH-rohs)

Take the garbage containers to the dump.

Lleve los contenedores de basura al tiradero.

(YEH-beh lohs kohn-teh-neh-THOR-
ess deh bah-SOO-rah ahl
tee-rah-THEH-roh)

Recycle these items.

Recicle estas cosas.

(reh-SEE-kleh eh-stahs KOH-sahs)

Put items for recycling <u>here</u>.

Ponga <u>aquí</u> los artículos para el reciclaje.

(POHNG-gah ah-kee lohs ahr-TEE-
koo-lohs pah-rah el
reh-see-KLAH-heh)

in this <u>basket</u>

en esta <u>canasta</u>

(en EH-stah kah-NAH-stah)

box

caja

(KAH-hah)

bag

bolsa

(BOHL-sah)

Food Service

Great food service is an earmark of a good hotel. These phrases will help you ensure that your policies are carried out.

Room Service

Put these items on the cart.	**Ponga estas cosas en la carretilla.** (POHNG-gah eh-stahs KOH-sahs en lah kahr-reh-TEE-yah)
Check to see if the tray includes napkins for each guest in the room.	**Cheque que hay servilletas para todos los huéspedes de la habitación.** (CHEH-keh keh eye sehr-bee-YEH-tahs pah-rah toh-thos lohs WESS-peh-thess deh lah ah-bee-tah-S'YOHN)
a knife	**un cuchillo** (oon koo-CHEE-yoh)
a fork	**un tenedor** (oon teh-neh-THOR)
a spoon	**una cuchara** (oo-nah koo-CHAH-rah)
salt and pepper	**sal y pimienta** (sahl ee peem-YEN-tah)
water	**agua** (AH-gwah)
water glasses	**vasos para agua** (BAH-sohs pah-rah AH-gwah)

Be careful not to spill anything.	**Cuidado de no derramar nada.**
	(kwee-THAH-thoh deh noh dehr-rah-MAHR NAH-thah)
Make sure everything is on a flat surface.	**Asegúrese de que todo esté en una superficie plana.**
	(ah-seh-GOO-reh-seh deh keh toh-thoh eh-STEH en oo-nah soo-pehr-FEESE-yeh PLAH-nah)
Take the cart to Room 302.	**Lleve la carretilla a la habitición 302.**
	(YEH-beh lah kahr-reh-TEE-yah ah lah ah-bee-tah-S'YOHN TRESS SEH-roh DOHS)
Use the service elevator.	**Use el ascensor de servicio.**
	(OO-seh el ah-sen-SOR deh sehr-BEESE-yoh)
If you spill something, return to the kitchen for a replacement.	**Si algo se derrama, vuelva a la cocina para reemplazarlo.**
	(see AHL-goh seh deh-RAH-mah B'WELL-bah ah lah koh-SEE-nah pah-rah reh-em-plah-SAHR-loh)
Knock on the guest's door.	**Toque a la puerta del huésped.**
	(TOH-keh ah lah P'WEHR-tah del WESS-ped)
Say "Room Service."	**Diga "Room Service".**
	(DEE-gah "Room Service")
Be courteous to the guest.	**Sea cordial con el huésped.**
	(SEH-ah kord-YAHL kohn el WESS-ped)

Push the cart into the room.	**Entre al cuarto con la carretilla.**
	(EN-treh ahl KWAHR-toh kohn lah kahr-reh-TEE-yah)
Put the tray on the table.	**Ponga la bandeja en la mesa.**
	(POHNG-gah lah bahn-deh-hah en lah MEH-sah)
Ask "Is your order correct?"	**Pregunte "Is your order correct?"**
	(pre-GOON-teh "Is your order correct?")
If there is a mistake, return to the kitchen for a replacement.	**Si hay un error, vuelva a la cocina para hacer el cambio.**
	(see eye-oon ehr-ROR B'WELL-bah ah lah koh-SEE-nah pah-rah ah-SEHR el KAHMB-yoh)
say "I'm very sorry."	**diga "I'm very sorry".**
	(DEE-gah "I'm very sorry")
Leave promptly.	**Salga en seguida.**
	(SAHL-gah en seh-GHEE-thah)
When the guests have finished eating . . .	**Cuando los huéspedes hayan terminado de comer...**
	(kwahn-doh lohs WESS-peh-thess EYE-ahn tehr-mee-NAH-thoh deh koh-MEHR)
Retrieve the food and beverage trays.	**Recoja las bandejas.**
	(reh-KOH-hah lahs bahn-deh-hahs)
Return the trays to the kitchen.	**Devuelva las bandejas a la cocina.**
	(deh-B'WELL-bah lahs bahn-deh-hahs ah lah koh-SEE-nah)

Report any problems to your supervisor.

Reporte cualquier problema a su supervisor.

(reh-por-teh kwal-k'YEHR proh-BLEH-mah ah soo soo-pehr-bee-SOR)

Banquet Setup

In this section you will find phrases that will help you explain how to set up a party room for a banquet.

Clear the room of furniture.

Saque todos los muebles del salón.

(SAH-keh TOH-thohs lohs M'WEH-bless del sah-LOHN)

Sweep the floor.

Barra el piso.

(BAHR-rah el PEE-soh)

Mop the floor.

Pase el trapeador por el piso.

(PAH-seh el trah-peh-ah-THOR por el PEE-soh)

Report any necessary repairs.

Reporte cualquier cosa que esté rota o que no funcione.

(reh-por-teh kwahl-K'YEHR koh-sah keh eh-steh ROH-tah oh keh noh foon-S'YOH-neh)

Set up thirty tables for eight people each.

Ponga treinta mesas para ocho personas cada una.

(POHNG-gah TRAYN-tah MEH-sahs pah-rah oh-choh pehr-SOH-nahs kah-thah OO-nah)

Make sure there are eight chairs at each table.	**Cheque que hay a ocho sillas para cada mesa.**
	(CHEH-keh keh EYE-yah OH-choh SEE-yahs pa-rah KAH-thah MEH-sah)
Fold the napkins, like this.	**Doble las servilletas, así.**
	(DOH-bleh lahs sehr-bee-YEH-tahs ah-SEE)
Set each place with a napkin.	**Coloque en cada sitio una servilleta.**
	(koh-LOH-keh en kah-thah SEET-yoh oo-nah sehr-bee-YEH-tah)
a knife	**un cuchillo**
	(oon koo-CHEE-yoh)
a fork	**un tenedor**
	(oon teh-neh-THOR)
a spoon	**una cuchara**
	(oo-nah koo-CHAH-rah)
a salad fork	**un tenedor para ensaladas**
	(oon teh-neh-THOR pah-rah en-sah-LAH-thahs)
a dessert spoon	**una cuchara para el postre**
	(oo-nah koo-CHAH-rah pah-rah el POH-streh)
a water glass	**un vaso para agua**
	(oon BAH-soh pah-rah AH-gwah)
two wine glasses	**dos copas para vino**
	(DOHS KOH-pahs pah-rah BEE-noh)

a champagne glass	**una copa para champaña**
	(oo-nah KOH-pah pah-rah
	chahm-PAHN-yah)
a <u>dinner</u> plate	**un plato <u>plano</u>**
	(oon PLAH-toh PLAH-noh)
salad	**para la ensalada**
	(pah-rah lah en-sah-LAH-thah)
a basket of bread	**una cesta con pan**
	(oo-nah SEH-stah kohn PAHN)
a menu	**un menú**
	(oon meh-NOO)
a party favor	**un recuerdo de la fiesta**
	(oon reh-KWEHR-doh deh lah
	F'YES-tah)
a company brochure	**un folleto de la compañía**
	(oon foh-YEH-toh deh lah
	kohm-pahn-YEE-ah)
a small vase of flowers	**un pequeño arreglo de flores**
	(oon peh-KEN-yoh ahr-REH-
	gloh deh FLOH-ress)
a rose	**una rosa**
	(oo-nah ROH-sah)
Place a <u>floral arrangement</u> in the center of the table.	**Coloque <u>un arreglo de flores</u> en el centro de la mesa.**
	(koh-LOH-keh oon ahr-REH-gloh deh
	FLOH-ress en el SEN-troh deh lah
	MEH-sah)
the table number	**el número de la mesa**
	(el NOO-meh-roh deh lah
	MEH-sah)

two candlesticks with candles

dos candelabros con velas

(DOHS cahn-deh-LAH-brohs
kohn BEH-lahs)

Place a sugar bowl on each table.

Coloque un azucarero en cada mesa.

(koh-LOH-keh oon ah-soo-kah-REH-
roh en kah-thah MEH-sah)

salt and pepper shakers

un salero y un pimentero

(oon sah-LEH-roh ee oon
pee-men-TEH-roh)

a butter dish

una mantequillera

(oo-nah mahn-teh-kee-YEH-rah)

ashtrays

ceniceros

(seh-nee-SEH-rohs)

matchbooks

libritos de cerillos

(lee-BREE-tohs deh
seh-REE-yohs)

Fill the water glasses.

Llene los vasos con agua.

(YEH-neh lohs BAH-sohs kohn
AH-gwah)

Light the candles at seven P.M.

Encienda las velas a las siete de la noche.

(en-S'YEN-dah lahs BEH-lahs ah lahs
S'YEH-teh deh lah NOH-cheh)

Set up five buffet tables.

Ponga cinco mesas para el bufé.

(POHNG-gah SEENG-koh MEH-sahs
pah-rah el boo-FEH)

a service table

una mesa de servicio

(oo-nah MEH-sah deh
sehr-BEE-s'yoh)

a table for <u>the main courses</u>

una mesa para <u>los platos</u>
  <u>principales</u>
(oo-nah MEH-sah pah-rah
  lohs PLAH-tohs preen-see-
  PAH-less)

the salads

las ensaladas
(lahs en-sah-LAH-thahs)

the desserts

los postres
(lohs POH-stress)

coffee and tea

café y té
(kah-FEH ee TEH)

a bar

una barra
(oo-nah BAHR-rah)

a dance floor

una pista de baile
(oo-nah PEE-stah deh BYE-leh)

a bandstand

una plataforma para la banda
(oo-nah plah-tah-FOR-mah
  pah-rah lah BAHN-dah)

Set up <u>the microphones</u>.

Instale <u>los micrófonos</u>.
(een-STAH-leh lohs
  mee-KROH-foh-nohs)

the speakers

los parlantes
(lohs pahr-LAHN-tess)

special lighting

las luces especiales
(lahs LOO-sess
  eh-spess-YAH-less)

Banquet Service

Be attentive to the guests' needs.

Ponga atención a las necesidades de los huéspedes.

(POHNG-gah ah-ten-S'YOHN ah lahs neh-seh-see-THAH-thess deh lohs WESS-peh-thess)

Serve all guests at each table within two minutes.

Sirva a todos los huéspedes de cada mesa dentro de dos minutos.

(SEER-bah ah toh-thohs lohs WESS-peh-thess deh kah-thah MEH-sah den-troh deh DOHS mee-NOO-tohs)

Serve each guest from the left.

Sirva a cada huésped desde el lado izquierdo.

(SEER-bah ah kah-thah WESS-ped des-deh el LAH-tho eese-K'YEHR-doh)

Refill the water glasses often.

Rellene los vasos con agua a menudo.

(re-YEH-neh lohs BAH-sohs kohn AH-gwah ah meh-NOO-thoh)

the wine glasses

las copas

(lahs KOH-pahs)

the coffee cups

las tazas de café

(lahs TAH-sahs deh kah-FEH)

the tea cups

las tazas de té

(lahs TAH-sahs deh TEH)

when empty

cuando estén vacías

(kwahn-doh eh-STEN bah-SEE-ahs)

Specific Instructions for Kitchen and Food Service Staff

Watch the guests to see if they are finished eating.

Observe a los huéspedes para ver si han terminado de comer.

(ohb-SEHR-beh ah lohs WESS-peh-thess pah-rah behr see ahn tehr-mee-NAH-thoh deh koh-MEHR)

Remove the plates from the right.

Retire los platos desde el lado derecho.

(reh-TEE-reh lohs PLAH-tohs des-deh el LAH-thoh deh-REH-choh)

Remove all plates before the next course is served.

Retire todos los platos de la mesa antes de servir el plato siguiente.

(reh-TEE-reh TOH-thohs lohs PLAH-tohs deh lah MEH-sah ahn-tess deh sehr-BEER el PLAH-toh seeg-YEN-teh)

If someone drops a fork, replace it with a clean one.

Si alguien pierde un tenedor, reemplácelo con uno nuevo.

(see ahl-g'yen P'YEHR-deh oon teh-neh-THOR reh-em-PLAH-seh-loh kohn oo-noh N'WEH-boh)

knife

un cuchillo

(oon koo-CHEE-yoh)

spoon

una cuchara

(oo-nah koo-CHAH-rah)

napkin

una servilleta

(oo-nah sehr-bee-YEH-tah)

If there is a spill . . .	**Si alguien derrama algo...**
	(see ahl-g'yen dehr-RAH-mah AHL-goh)
clean it up right away.	**límpielo en seguida.**
	(LEEMP-yeh-loh en seh-GHEE-thah)
assist the guest with soiled clothing.	**ayude al huésped a quitar las manchas de la ropa.**
	(ah-YOO-theh ahl-WESS-ped ah kee-TAHR lahs MAHN-chahs deh lah ROH-pah)
place clean napkins over wet spots.	**coloque unas servilletas limpias sobre las manchas mojadas**.
	(koh-LOH-keh oo-nahs sehr-bee-YEH-tahs LEEM-p'yahs soh-breh lahs MAHN-chahs moh-HAH-thahs)
Promptly remove the dishes as guests complete each course.	**Después que los huéspedes terminen cada plato, retire los platos en seguida.**
	(dess-PWESS keh lohs WESS-peh-thess tehr-MEE-nen kah-thah PLAH-toh reh-TEE-reh-lohs PLAH-tohs en seh-GHEE-thah)
Take the dirty dishes to the kitchen right away.	**Lleve los platos sucios a la cocina en seguida.**
	(YEH-beh lohs PLAH-tohs SOOSE-yohs ah lah koh-SEE-nah en seh-GHEE-thah)

f Public Rooms

t will help you explain the tasks you expect
o to routinely to keep the hotel in good

Saque toda la basura.
(SAH-keh TOH-thah lah bah-SOO-rah)
Vacíe los ceniceros.
(bah-SEE-eh lohs seh-nee-SEH-rohs)
Lave
(LAH-beh)

kitchen. **Lleve los platos usados a la cocina.**
(YEH-beh lohs PLAH-tohs
oo-SAH-thohs ah lah koh-SEE-nah)
los vasos
(lohs BAH-sohs)
**Pase la aspiradora por los pasillos
públicos.**
(PAH-seh lah ah-spee-rah-THOR-ah
por lohs pah-SEE-yohs
POO-blee-kohs)
los salones para reuniones
(lohs sah-LOH-ness pah-rah
reh'oon-YOH-ness)
los salones de baile
(lohs sah-LOH-ness deh
BYE-leh)
los pisos de los ascensores
(lohs PEE-sohs deh lohs
ah-sen-SOR-ess)

Work quietly.

Trabaje sin hacer ruido.
(trah-BAH-heh seen ah-sehr
R'WEE-thoh)

Do not rattle the plates.

No haga ruido con los platos.
(NOH AH-gah R'WEE-thoh kohn lohs
PLAH-tohs)

glasses

los vasos
(lohs BAH-sohs)

silverware

los cubiertos
(lohs koob-YEHR-tohs)

Banquet Cleanup

When the meeting has
concluded . . .

**Cuando se haya terminado la
reunión...**
(kwahn-doh seh ah-yah tehr-mee-
NAH-thoh lah reh-oo-N'YOHN)

reset the banquet room
according to your
supervisor's specifications.

**arregle el salón según las
instrucciones de su
supervisor.**
(ahr-REH-gleh el sah-LOHN
seh-goon lahs een-strook-
S'YOH-ness deh soo
soo-pehr-bee-SOR)

return the used items to
the storage closet.

**devuelva al armario los
artículos utilizados para
el banquete.**
(de-BWELL-bah ahl ahr-MAHR-
yoh lohs ahr-TEE-koo-lohs
oo-tee-lee-SAH-thohs pah-
rah el bahng-keh-teh)

113

put the room back as it was
before.

**arregle el salón como estaba
antes.**
(ahr-REH-gleh el sah-LOHN
koh-moh eh-stah-bah
AHN-tess)

maintain the established
cleaning schedule.

**mantenga el horario
establecido para la
limpieza.**
(mahn-TENG-gah el or-AHR-yoh
eh-stah-bleh-SEE-thoh pah-
rah lah leemp-YEH-sah)

keep the rooms presentable
at all times.

**mantenga los salones en
buen orden en todo
momento.**
(mahn-TENG-gah lohs sah-LOH-
ness en b'wen OR-den en
TOH-thoh moh-MEN-toh)

Routine Cle

Here are some p
your cleaning cr
shape.

Remove all the tras

<u>Empty</u> the ashtrays

Wash

Take any used <u>dishe</u>

n this sectio
maintenance

The English
Spanish:

maintenance

From that, w

the maintenance

the maintenance

glasses

Vacuum the <u>public h</u>

conference roor

ballrooms

elevator floors

Specific Tasks for the Indoor Maintenance Team

Mop the elevator floors.

Pase el trapeador por los pisos de los ascensores.
(PAH-seh el trah-peh-ah-THOR por lohs PEE-sohs deh lohs ah-sen-SOR-ess)

Dust all the furniture.

Pásele el trapo por todos los muebles.
(PAH-seh-leh el TRAH-poh por TOH-thohs lohs M'WEH-bless)

Polish

Lustre
(LOOSE-treh)

Wipe the light fixtures.

Límpie las lámparas con un trapo.
(LEEMP-yeh lahs LAHM-pah-rahs kohn oon TRAH-poh)

Shine the brass fittings.

Pula los accesorios de bronce.
(POO-lah lohs ahk-seh-SOR-yohs deh BROHN-seh)

Wipe off any fingerprints from any surface.

Limpie las huellas digitales de cualquier superficie.
(LEEMP-yeh lahs WEH-yahs dee-hee-TAH-less deh kwahl-k'yehr soo-pehr-FEESE-yeh)

Inspect the elevators.

Cheque los ascensores.
(CHEH-keh lohs ah-sen-SOR-ess)

Wipe the elevator controls.

Limpie los botones de control de los ascensores.
(LEEMP-yeh lohs boh-TOH-ness deh kohn-TROHL deh lohs ah-sen-SOR-ess)

Inspect the public restrooms frequently.

Cheque los baños públicos frecuentemente.
(CHEH-keh lohs BAHN-yohs POO-blee-kohs freh-kwen-teh-MEN-teh)

Clean the toilets.

Limpie los inodoros.
(LEEMP-yeh lohs ee-noh-THOR-ohs)

sinks

los lavabos
(lohs lah-BAH-bohs)

Wash the floors.

Lave el piso.
(LAH-beh el PEE-soh)

Check the supply of hand soap.

Fíjese en la cantidad de jabón líquido.
(FEE-heh-seh en la kahn-tee-THAD deh hah-BOHN LEE-kee-thoh)

paper towels

toallas de papel
(toh-AH-yahs deh pah-PELL)

Kleenex

pañuelos de papel
(pahn-Y'WEH lohs deh-pah-PELL)

Make sure all surfaces are clean and dry.

Cheque que todas las superficies estén limpias y secas.
(CHEH-keh keh toh-thahs lahs soo-pehr-FEESE-yehs eh-STEN LEEMP-yahs ee SEH-kahs)

Tools and Equipment

Here are the words and phrases for common cleaning equipment and supplies.

Specific Tasks for the Indoor Maintenance Team

Maintenance equipment and supplies are kept in the basement.

Los productos y los equipos para el mantenimiento están en el sótano.

(lohs proh-THOOK-tohs ee lohs eh-KEE-pohs pah-rah el mahn-ten-ee-M'YEN-toh eh-stahn en el SOH-tah-noh)

Use this product.

Use este producto.

(oo-seh EH-steh proh-THOOK-toh)

this cleaner

este limpiador

(eh-steh leemp-yah-THOR)

Windex

Windex

(WEEN-deh)

wax

cera

(SEH-rah)

floor polish

lustrador de suelos

(loose-trah-THOR deh SWEH-lohs)

furniture polish

cera para muebles

(SER-rah pah-rah M'WEH-bless)

a wet mop

un trapeador mojado

(oon trah-peh-ah-THOR moh-HAH-thoh)

dry

seco

(SEH-koh)

a bucket

una cubeta

(oo-nah koo-BEH-tah)

the vacuum cleaner

la aspiradora

(lah ah-spee-rah-THOR-ah)

these rags

estos trapos

(EH-stohs TRAH-pohs)

a damp cloth	**un trapo mojado** (oon TRAH-poh moh-HAH-thoh)
a dry cloth	**un trapo seco** (oon TRAH-poh SEH-koh)
a floor polisher	**una máquina para encerar** **pisos** (oo-nah MAH-kee-nah pah-rah en-seh-RAHR PEE-sohs)

Keeping the Hotel in Good Repair

These are phrases for explaining the kinds of general repairs that might need to be done.

Keep the hotel in good repair.	**Mantenga el hotel en buenas** **condiciones.** (mahn-TENG-gah el oh-TELL en BWEH-nahs kohn dee-S'YOH-ness)

Routine Tasks for the Maintenance Team

Inspect the bathroom pipes frequently.	**Haga frecuentes inspecciones** **de las cañerías de los baños.** (AH-gah freh-KWEN-tess een-spek- S'YOH-ness deh lahs kahn-yeh- REE-ahs deh lohs BAHN-yohs)
heating system	**del sistema de calefacción** (del see-STEH-mah deh kah-lee-fahk-S'YOHN)

Specific Tasks for the Indoor Maintenance Team

air conditioning system	**del sistema de aire acondicionado** (del sees-TEH-mah deh EYE-reh ah-kohn-dee-s'yoh-NAH-thoh)
Change the furnace filters once a month.	**Cambie los filtros de la calefacción una vez al mes.** (KAHM-b'yeh lohs FEEL-trohs deh lah kah-leh-fak-S'YOHN oo-nah bess ahl MESS)
Check to see that the drains are clear.	**Cheque que los desagües no estén bloqueados.** (CHEH-keh keh lohs dess-AH-gwess noh eh-STEN bloh-keh-AH-thohs)
Replace all burned-out light bulbs.	**Reemplace las bombillas quemadas.** (reh-em-PLAH-seh lahs bohm-BEE-yahs keh-MAH-thahs)
Re-caulk the bathtubs.	**Enmasille las bañeras.** (ehn-mah-SEE-yeh lahs bahn-YEH-rahs)
sinks	**los lavabos** (lohs lah-BAH-bohs)
toilets	**los inodoros** (lohs ee-noh-THOH-rohs)

Special Projects for the Maintenance Team

Here are phrases that detail some of the maintenance problems that may crop up from time to time.

Be on call to <u>make repairs</u>.	**Esté listo para <u>hacer reparaciones</u>.**
	(eh-steh LEE-stoh pah-rah ah-sehr reh-pah-rah-S'YOH-ness)
fix minor problems	**arreglar problemas menores**
	(ahr-reh-GLAHR proh-BLEH-mahs meh-NOR-ess)
Repair the broken <u>light fixture</u>.	**Repare <u>la lámpara</u> rota.**
	(reh-PAH-reh lah LAHM-pah-rah ROH-tah)
lamp	**la lámpara** (yes, it's the same word!)
	(lah LAHM-pah-rah)
window	**la ventana**
	(lah ben-TAH-nah)
window pane	**el vidrio**
	(el BEETHE-r'yoh)
table	**la mesa**
	(lah MEH-sah)
chair	**la silla**
	(lah SEE-yah)
easy chair	**el sillón**
	(el see-YOHN)
bed	**la cama**
	(lah KAH-mah)
door lock	**la cerradura de la puerta**
	(lah sehr-rah-THOO-rah deh lah PWEHR-tah)
television set	**el televisor**
	(el teh-leh-bee-SOR)
remote control	**el control remoto**
	(el kohn-TROHL reh-MOH-toh)

Specific Tasks for the Indoor Maintenance Team

hair dryer	**el secador**
	(el seh-kah-THOR)
iron	**la plancha**
	(lah PLAHN-chah)
ironing board	**el burro de planchar**
	(el BOOR-roh deh
	plahn-CHAHR)
vacuum cleaner	**la aspiradora**
	(lah ah-spee-rah-THOR-ah)
room heater	**la calefacción**
	(lah kah-leh-fahk-S'YOHN)
air conditioner	**el aire acondicionador**
	(el EYE-reh ah-kohn-dee-s'yoh-
	nah-THOR)
vent	**el escape**
	(el eh-SKAH-peh)
telephone	**el teléfono**
	(el teh-LEH-foh-noh)
electrical wiring	**la instalación eléctrica**
	(lah een-stah-lah-S'YOHN
	eh-LEK-tree-kah)
stopped-up <u>sink</u>	**el lavabo bloqueado**
	(el lah-BAH-boh
	bloh-keh-AH-thoh)
bathtub	**la bañera**
	(lah bahn-YEH-rah)
shower	**la ducha**
	(lah DOO-chah)
toilet	**el inodoro**
	(el een-oh-THOH-roh)

Tools and Equipment

These phrases will help you tell those on your maintenance team what tools and products you would like them to use.

caulking	**masilla**
	(mah-SEE-yah)
drain cleaner	**limpiador de desagües**
	(leemp-yah-THOR deh
	dess-AH-gwess)
these filters	**estos filtros**
	(EH-stohs FEEL-trohs)
seventy-five-watt light bulbs	**bombillas de setenta y cinco vatios**
	(bohm-BEE-yahs deh seh-TEN-tah ee
	SEENG-koh BAHT-yohs)
Use these tools.	**Use estas herramientas.**
	(OO-seh EH-stahs ehr-rahm-YEN-tahs)
a ladder	**una escalera de mano**
	(oo-nah eh-skah-LEH-rah deh
	MAH-noh)
a toolbox	**una caja de herramientas**
	(oo-nah KAH-hah deh
	ehr-rah-M'YEN-tahs)
a screwdriver	**un destornillador**
	(oon dess-tor-nee-yah-THOR)
a Phillips head screwdriver	**un destornillador de punta**
	de cruz
	(oon dess-tohr-nee-yah-THOR
	deh POON-tah deh
	KROOSE)

Specific Tasks for the Indoor Maintenance Team

screws	**tornillos**
	(tor-NEE-yohs)
a hammer	**un martillo**
	(oon mahr-TEE-yoh)
nails	**clavos**
	(KLAH-bohs)
an (electric) drill	**un taladro (eléctrico)**
	(oon tah-lah-droh
	[eh-LEK-tree-koh])
pliers	**alicates**
	(ah-lee-KAH-tess)
vise grips	**pinzas perras**
	(PEEN-sahs PEHR-rahs)
a wrench	**una llave**
	(oo-nah YAH-beh)
a utility knife	**una navaja**
	(oo-nah nah-BAH-hah)
a solderer	**un soldador**
	(oon sohl-dah-THOR)
a stapler	**una grapadora**
	(oo-nah grah-pah-THOR-ah)
a plumber's wrench	**una llave inglesa**
	(oo-nah YAH-beh
	eeng-GLEH-sah)
a plunger	**un destapador**
	(oon dess-tah-pah-THOR)
a washer	**una arandela**
	(oo-nah ah-rahn-DEH-lah)
a snake (for drains)	**una serpiente**
	(oo-nah sehr-P'YEN-teh)

Pest Control

In this section you will find phrases that deal with avoiding and trapping pests.

If you see rodents, set traps.	**Si ve roedores, ponga trampas.** (see beh roh-eh-THOR-ess POHNG-gah TRAHM-pahs)
mice	**ratones** (rah-TOH-ness)
rats	**ratas** (RAH-tahs)
insects	**insectos** (een-SEK-tohs)
ants	**hormigas** (or-MEE-gahs)
spiders	**arañas** (ah-RAHN-yahs)
cockroaches	**cucarachas** (koo-kah-RAH-chahs)
pests	**animales indeseables** (ah-nee-MAH-less een-deh-seh-AH-bless)
Remove the dead animals.	**Saque los animales muertos.** (SAH-keh lohs ah-nee-mah-less M'WEHR-tohs)
Use this insecticide.	**Use este insecticida.** (oo-seh EH-steh een-sek-tee- SEE-thah)

Specific Tasks for the Indoor Maintenance Team

Call for help if you need it.

Pida ayuda si la necesita.

(PEE-thah ah-YOO-thah see lah
neh-seh-SEE-tah)

Report serious problems to
your supervisor.

**Reporte cualquier problema serio
a su supervisor.**

(re-por-teh kwahl-k'yehr
proh-bleh-mah SEHR-yoh ah soo
soo-pehr-bee-SOR)

Appendix

Numbers

0	**cero**	20	**veinte**
1	**uno**	21	**veintiuno**
2	**dos**	22	**veintidós**
3	**tres**	23	**veintitrés**
4	**cuatro**	24	**veinticuatro**
5	**cinco**	25	**veinticinco**
6	**seis**	26	**veintiséis**
7	**siete**	27	**veintisiete**
8	**ocho**	28	**veintiocho**
9	**nueve**	29	**veintinueve**
10	**diez**	30	**treinta**
11	**once**	31	**treinta y uno**
12	**doce**	32	**treinta y dos**
13	**trece**	33	**treinta y tres**
14	**catorce**	34	**treinta y cuatro**
15	**quince**	35	**treinta y cinco**
16	**dieciséis**	36	**treinta y seis**
17	**diecisiete**	37	**treinta y siete**
18	**dieciocho**	38	**treinta y ocho**
19	**diecinueve**	39	**treinta y nueve**

40	**cuarenta**	70	**setenta**
41	**cuarenta y uno**	71	**setenta y uno**
42	**cuarenta y dos**	72	**setenta y dos**
43	**cuarenta y tres**	73	**setenta y tres**
44	**cuarenta y cuatro**	74	**setenta y cuatro**
45	**cuarenta y cinco**	75	**setenta y cinco**
46	**cuarenta y seis**	76	**setenta y seis**
47	**cuarenta y siete**	77	**setenta y siete**
48	**cuarenta y ocho**	78	**setenta y ocho**
49	**cuarenta y nueve**	79	**setenta y nueve**
50	**cincuenta**	80	**ochenta**
51	**cincuenta y uno**	81	**ochenta y uno**
52	**cincuenta y dos**	82	**ochenta y dos**
53	**cincuenta y tres**	83	**ochenta y tres**
54	**cincuenta y cuatro**	84	**ochenta y cuatro**
55	**cincuenta y cinco**	85	**ochenta y cinco**
56	**cincuenta y seis**	86	**ochenta y seis**
57	**cincuenta y siete**	87	**ochenta y siete**
58	**cincuenta y ocho**	88	**ochenta y ocho**
59	**cincuenta y nueve**	89	**ochenta y nueve**
60	**sesenta**	90	**noventa**
61	**sesenta y uno**	91	**noventa y uno**
62	**sesenta y dos**	92	**noventa y dos**
63	**sesenta y tres**	93	**noventa y tres**
64	**sesenta y cuatro**	94	**noventa y cuatro**
65	**sesenta y cinco**	95	**noventa y cinco**
66	**sesenta y seis**	96	**noventa y seis**
67	**sesenta y siete**	97	**noventa y siete**
68	**sesenta y ocho**	98	**noventa y ocho**
69	**sesenta y nueve**	99	**noventa y nueve**

Appendix

100	**cien**	200	**doscientos**
101	**ciento uno**	300	**trescientos**
102	**ciento dos**	400	**cuatrocientos**
114	**ciento catorce**	500	**quinientos**
129	**ciento veintinueve**	600	**seiscientos**
133	**ciento treinta y tres**	700	**setecientos**
142	**ciento cuarenta y dos**	800	**ochocientos**
156	**ciento cincuenta y seis**	900	**novecientos**
		1000	**mil**
167	**ciento sesenta y siete**	2000	**dos mil**
179	**ciento setenta y nueve**	2009	**dos mil nueve**
		40,000	**cuarenta mil**
188	**ciento ochenta y ocho**	1999	**mil novecientos noventa y nueve**
194	**ciento noventa y cuatro**	1,000,000	**un millón**

English-Spanish Glossary

Expressions

A.M.	de la mañana
Be careful.	Cuidado. / Tenga cuidado.
Call 911.	Llame al nueve-uno-uno.
Don't . . .	No...
Excuse me.	Disculpe.
For how long . . .	¿Por cuánto tiempo... ?
God willing!	¡Ojalá!
Good afternoon.	Buenas tardes.
Good evening.	Buenas tardes / noches.
Good morning.	Buenos días.
Good night.	Buenas noches.
Good-bye.	Adiós.
Hello.	Hola.
How . . . ?	¿Cómo… ?
How are you?	¿Cómo está usted?
How do you say . . . ?	¿Cómo se dice... ?
How many . . . ?	¿Cuántos... ?
How much . . . ?	¿Cuánto... ?
How . . . ?	¿Cómo... ?
How . . . ?	¿Qué... ?
I'm sorry.	Lo siento.
No.	No.
Please.	Por favor.
P.M.	de la tarde / de la noche
See you later.	Hasta luego.
Thank you.	Gracias.
Until when . . . ?	¿Hasta cuándo... ?
Welcome.	Bienvenido.
What . . . ?	¿Cuál... ?
What . . . ?	¿Qué... ?

What for . . . ?	¿Para qué... ?
When . . . ?	¿Cuándo... ?
Where . . . ?	¿Dónde... ?
Where from . . . ?	¿De dónde... ?
Where to . . . ?	¿Adónde... ?
Who . . . ?	¿Quién... ?
Who with . . . ?	¿Con quién... ?
Whose . . . ?	¿De quién... ?
Why . . . ?	¿Por qué?
Yes.	Sí.
You're welcome.	De nada.

People

boss	jefe / patrón
boyfriend	novio
brother	hermano
buser	ayudante de mesero
child	niño, niña
children	niños, niñas
children (sons and daughters)	hijos, hijas
cleaning staff	personal para limpieza
cook	cocinero /cocinera
daughter	hija
dishwasher	lavaplatos
employee	empleado (-a), (-os), (-as) / personal
father	papá / padre
friend	amigo, amiga
girlfriend	novia
guest	huésped
he	él
her	la / le / a ella
him	lo / le / a él
husband	esposo
I	yo
kitchen staff	personal para la cocina
laundry worker	lavandero / lavandera
maintenance specialist	encargado del servicio de mantenimiento
mother	mamá / madre
neighbor	vecino, vecina
parents	padres
reference	referencia

she	ella
sister	hermana
someone	alguien
son	hijo
staff	personal
they	ellos / ellas
VIP	persona importante
we	nosotros / nosotras
wife	esposa
you	usted
you all	ustedes

Places

back door	puerta de atrás
basement	sótano
bathroom	baño
bedroom	dormitorio / cuarto / recámara
bus stop	parada de autobuses
closet (clothes)	guardarropa
closet (linen)	armario para la ropa blanca
closet (storage)	armario
dining room	comedor
floor (of a building)	piso
front door	puerta princial
garage	garaje
guest room	habitación para huéspedes
gym	gimnasio
hall	pasillo
hotel	hotel
kitchen	cocina
laundry room	lavandería
lobby	lobby
pantry	despensa
place	lugar
playroom	cuarto de recreo
pool	piscina
public areas	áreas públicas
restaurant	restaurante
room	habitación
service entrance	entrada de servicio
suite	suite
swimming pool	piscina

Words That Describe People, Places, or Things

(Note: the endings of these words may change to match the gender or number of the words they describe)

attentive	atento (-a), (-os), (-as)
bad	malo (-a), (-os), (-as)
big	grande, grandes
broken	roto (-a), (-os), (-as)
burned-out (bulb)	quemada
clean	limpio (-a), (-os), (-as)
clear (drain)	no bloqueado (-a), (-os), (-as)
cloudy	nublado
cold	frío (-a), (-os), (-as)
comfortable	cómodo (-a), (-os), (-as)
cool	templado
courteous	cordial, cordiales
damaged	dañado (-a), (-os), (-as)
damp	húmedo (-a), (-os), (-as)
dangerous	peligroso (-a), (-os), (-as)
dark	oscuro (-a), (-os), (-as)
dead	muerto (-a), (-os), (-as)
dirty	sucio (-a), (-os), (-as)
double	doble
dry	seco (-a), (-os), (-as)
dry-cleaned	limpiado en seco
efficient	eficiente
empty	vacío (-a), (-os), (-as)
fine (small)	fino (-a), (-os), (-as)
fired (from a job)	despedido (-a), (-os), (-as)
five-star	de cinco estrellas
flat (shoes)	bajos
folded	doblado (-a), (-os), (-as)
fresh	fresco (-a), (-os), (-as)
good	bueno (-a), (-os), (-as)
healthy	saludable
heavy	pesado (-a), (-os), (-as)
high	alto (-a), (-os), (-as)
hired	contratado (-a), (-os), (-as)
hot (water, food, etc.)	caliente, calientes
hot (weather)	hace calor
important	importante, importantes

English-Spanish Glossary

interior	interior
jammed	trancado (-a), (-os), (-as)
little	pequeño (-a), (-os), (-as)
locked	cerrada con llave
low	bajo (-a), (-os), (-as)
meat (products)	cárnico (-a), (-os), (-as)
medium (temperature)	medio alta
minor	menor, menores
necessary	necesario (-a), (-os), (-as)
new	nuevo (-a), (-os), (-as)
old	viejo (-a), (-os), (-as), antiguo (-a), (-os), (-as)
open	abierto (-a), (-os), (-as)
personal	personal, personales
prepared	preparado (-a), (-os), (-as)
presentable	en buen orden
punctual	puntual, puntuales
raw	crudo (-a), (-os), (-as)
rubber	de hule / de goma
rubber-soled (shoes)	con suela de hule
serious	serio (-a), (-os), (-as)
sick	enfermo (-a), (-os), (-as)
single (room)	sencilla
slippery	resbaloso
small	pequeño (-a), (-os), (-as)
special	especial
strange	extraño (-a), (-os), (-as)
sturdy	fuerte, fuertes
sunny	hace sol
thick	grueso (-a), (-os), (-as)
thin (slices)	fino (-a), (-os), (-as)
unlocked	abierto (-a), (-os), (-as)
unnecessary	innecesario (-a), (-os), (-as)
unsafe	peligroso (-a), (-os), (-as)
upholstered	tapizado (-a), (-os), (-as)
urgent	urgente
used	usado (-a), (-os), (-as)
VIP	especial
vital	primordial
wet	mojado (-a), (-os), (-as)
white	blanco (-a), (-os), (-as)
whole	entero (-a), (-os), (-as)
windy	hace viento
wooden	de madera

Words That Tell *How*

carefully	con cuidado
courteously	con cortesía
fine (not sick)	bien
fine (weather)	buen tiempo
frequently	frecuentemente
halfway (to a place)	a medio camino
immediately	en seguida
promptly	en seguida
quietly	sin ruido
separately	por separado
slowly	lentamente
so-so	más o menos
well	bien

Words That Tell *When*

advance, in	por adelantado
always	siempre / en todo momento
at all times	en todo momento
early	temprano
every day	todos los días
late	tarde
later	más tarde
midnight	medianoche
never	nunca
noon	mediodía
now	ahora
on the dot	en punto
on time	puntual
P.M.	de la tarde / de la noche
promptly	cuanto antes
soon	pronto
today	hoy
until	hasta
while	mientras

Words That Tell *How Much* or *How Many*

a few	unos pocos, unas pocas
a little	un poco

little (amount)	poco
many	muchos (-as)
many times	muchas veces
one time	una vez
several	varios (-a), (-os), (-as)
too many	demasiados (-as)
two times	dos veces

Words That Tell *Where*

at	en
behind	detrás de
between	entre
down there	abajo
downstairs	abajo
far	lejos
here	aquí
home (at)	en casa
home (toward)	a casa
in	en
in back of	detrás de
in front of	delante de
left (direction)	a la izquierda
near	cerca
next to	al lado de
on	en
on top of	encima de
out of	fuera de
outside	afuera
over there	allí
right (direction)	a la derecha
there	ahí
through	por
under	por debajo de
underneath	debajo de
up there	arriba
upstairs	arriba

Words That Tell *Whose*

her	su, sus
hers	suyo (-a), (-os), (-as)

his	su, sus, suyo (-a), (-os), (-as)
mine	mío (-a), (-os), (-as)
my	mi, mis
our, ours	nuestro (-a), (-os), (-as)
own (belonging to)	propio (-a), (-os), (-as)
theirs	suyo (-a), (-os), (-as)
your	su, sus
yours	suyo (-a), (-os), (-as)

Little Words

alone	solo
at	en
because	porque
before	antes
depending	depende
extra	extra
first	primero
first (most important)	primordial
if	si
like this	así
like that	así
maybe	quizás
per	por
that	ese, esa
these	estas, estos
this	este, esta
those	esas, esos
to	a
with me	conmigo
with	con
without	sin

Activities

Note: In this section, the words for activities are given in their *infinitive* form, the basic dictionary form which does *not* indicate who is doing the action. In the text of the book, most of the "action words" are given in the command form, appropriate for giving instructions.

add (to something)	agregar / añadir
adjust	ajustar
administer	administrar
air out	airear
arrange	arreglar
arrive	llegar
ask (a question)	preguntar
ask for	pedir
assist	ayudar
bake	cocinar en el horno
be attentive	poner atención
be careful	tener cuidado
be courteous	ser cordial / tratar con cortesía
beat (eggs, batter)	batir
bend	agacharse
boil	hervir
braise	estofar
break	romper
bring	traer
broil	asar a la parrilla
burn	quemar
butter	untar
call	llamar
carry	llevar
caulk	enmasillar
change	cambiar
check	checar
chop	cortar
clean	limpiar
clear	limpiar
close	cerrar
come in	entrar
come	venir
contact	contactar
cool	dejar que se enfríe
cream (butter)	mezclar bien
cut	cortar
defrost	descongelar
distribute	distribuir
do	hacer
draw (close)	cerrar
drink	tomar / beber
drop	perder
dry-clean	limpiar en seco

English-Spanish Glossary

dust	pasarle el trapo a
empty	vaciar
enter	entrar
expect	esperar
fall	caerse
feed	alimentar
fill	llenar
find	encontrar
finish	terminar
fire	despedir
fix	arreglar
fold	doblar
follow	seguir
fry	freír
garnish	decorar
get hurt	lastimarse
get sick	enfermarse
give	dar
go	ir
go get	buscar
grab	agarrar
guide	guiar
hang	colgar
have	tener
have an accident	tener un accidente
help	ayudar
hire	contratar
hurt oneself	lastimarse
insert	meter
inspect	checar / hacer inspecciones
install	instalar
jam	trancarse
keep	guardar
kneel	arrodillar
knock	tocar a la puerta
leave (a place)	salir de
leave (something)	dejar
let (allow)	dejar que
lift	levantar
light (candles)	encender
load	cargar
lock	cerrar con llave
look for	buscar
loosen	soltar
lose	perder

English-Spanish Glossary

maintain	mantener
make	hacer
make (bed)	arreglar
make repairs	hacer reparaciones
make sure	asegurarse
marinate	adobar / dejar en adobo
mark	marcar
measure	medir
mix	mezclar
monitor	checar, fijarse en
mop	pasar el trapeador
need	necesitar
observe	observar
open	abrir
operate	operar
order	ordenar
organize	organizar
pack	empacar
pay	pagar
peel	pelar
pick up	recoger
place	colocar
polish (furniture)	lustrar
polish (metal)	pulir
pour	verter
prepare	preparar
provide	proporcionar
pull	jalar
push	empujar
push (a button)	apretar
put	poner
raise	aumentar
rattle	hacer ruido
record (in a ledger)	anotar
recycle	reciclar
refill	rellenar
refrigerate	dejar en el refrigerador
remove	quitar
remove (plates)	retirar
repair	reparar
replace	cambiar / reemplazar
report	reportar / informar
retrieve	recoger
return (something)	devolver
ring	tocar

roast	cocinar en el horno
roll (dough)	estirar
run (machine)	estar en marcha
run (go fast)	correr
scrub	fregar
see	ver
send	mandar
separate	separar
serve	servir
set (the table)	poner
set (a dial)	seleccionar
set up (tables)	poner
shine (metal)	pulir
show	mostrar
show how to	enseñar
sift	tamizar
sign in / out	firmar / escribir su nombre
slip	resbalarse
smoke	fumar
smooth	alisar
sort	separar
space	espaciar
spill	derramar
spot-clean	limpiar las manchas
spray	salpicar
stack	apilar
start	empezar
start (begin to operate)	poner en marcha
stand (tolerate)	aguantar
stir	remover
stop	parar
sweep	barrer
take (in a vehicle)	llevar
take off	sacar
take out	sacar
teach	enseñar
tell	decir
throw	tirar
tolerate	aguantar
touch	tocar
transfer	pasar
tuck in	meter debajo
turn	girar
turn off (electrical)	apagar
turn off (water)	cerrar la llave del agua

turn on (electrical)	encender
turn on (water)	abrir la llave del agua
understand	entender
untangle	desenredar
use	usar
vacuum	pasar la aspiradora
wait	esperar
wash	lavar
watch	observar
wear	llevar / usar
weigh	pesar
wipe	limpiar
wipe	pasarle el trapo por
work	trabajar
wrap	envolver

Things

accident	accidente
air conditioner	acondicionador de aire
alcohol	alcohol
ambulance	ambulancia
ant	hormiga
apron	delantal
area	área
ashtray	cenicero
assistance	ayuda
attitude	actitud
back door	puerta de atrás
bag	bolsa
baking pan	molde
bandstand	plataforma para la banda
banquet	banquete
bar (for drinks)	barra
baseboards	zócalos
basket	canasta / cesta
bathmat	tapete del baño
bathtub	bañera
batter	masa
bed	cama
bedding	ropa de cama
bedspread	cubrecama
bell	timbre
belongings	pertenencias

blanket	frazada
blanket folder	dobladora de frazadas
bleach	lejía
blender	batidor
blinds	persianas
blood	sangre
body lotion	loción para el cuerpo
book	libro
bottom sheet	sábana de abajo
box	caja
bracelet	pulsera
breadcrumbs	migas de pan
break (rest)	descanso
brochure	folleto
bucket	cubeta
bureau	cómoda
butter dish	mantequillera
butter	mantequilla
button	botón
cake	pastel
candle	vela
candlestick	candelabro
card	tarjeta
carpet	alfombra
cart	carretilla / carrito
cash	efectivo
category	categoría
caulking	masilla
cell phone	celular
chair	silla
chair, easy	sillón
check	cheque
chemical supplies	químicas
china	vajilla
chocolates	chocolates
chopper	picadora
chunk	trozo
cleaning supplies	limpiadores
clock	reloj
closet	guardarropa
clothing	ropa
cockroach	cucaracha
coffee	café
coffee maker	cafetera
colander	colador, escurridor

conditions	condiciones
controls	botones de control
conveyor belt	cinta transportadora
cookies	galletas
corner (of a sheet)	punta
cream	crema
creamer	sustituto de la crema
cup	taza
curtain	cortina
cycle	programa / ciclo
dance floor	pista de baile
dessert	postre
detergent	detergente
dial	indicador
dish	plato
dishwasher	lavaplatos
distributor	destribuidor
documents	documentos
door	puerta
doorknob	perilla
dough	masa
drain cleaner	limpiador de desagües
drains	desagües
drapes	cortinas gruesas
drawers	cajones
drill	taladro
drugs	drogas
dry mop	trapeador seco
dryer (for clothes)	secadora
dryer (for hair)	secador
earrings	aretes
easy chair	sillón
egg	huevo
egg white	clara
egg yolk	yema
elevator	ascensor
entrance	entrada
equipment	equipo
fabric softener	suavizante de telas
fabric	tela
fat (grease)	grasa
favor (party)	recuerdo
feeder	alimentador
feeder ribbon	cinta de alimentación
filter	filtro

filter bag	bolsa del filtro
finger	dedo
fingerprints	huellas digitales
first aid	primeros auxilios
fish	pescado
floor	suelo / piso
floor (of a building)	piso
floor polish	lustrador de suelos
floor polisher	máquina para encerar pisos
flour	harina
folder (machine)	dobladora
food	comida
foot of the bed	pie de la cama
fork	tenedor
freezer	congelador
front door	puerta principal
fruit	frutas
furniture	muebles
furniture polish	cera para muebles
garbage	basura / restos de comida
garnish	guarnición
glass (drinking)	vaso
glass (wine)	copa
gloves	guantes
grater	rallador
grease	grasa
hairnet	redecilla
hammer	martillo
hands	manos
heating system	sistema de calefacción
heating unit	calefacción
height	altura
help	ayuda
herbs	hierbas
hole	agujero
ingredients	ingredientes
insecticide	insecticida
insects	insectos
instructions	instrucciones
iron	plancha
ironer	planchadora
ironing board	burro de planchar
item	artículo
jewelry	joyas
job	trabajo

key	llave
knife	cuchillo
knife, utility	navaja
ladder	escalera de mano
lamp	lámpara
laundry	ropa sucia / ropa para lavar
laundry room	lavandería
laundry service	servicio de lavandería
lemon wedges	trozos de limón
lid	tapa
light	luz
light bulb	bombilla
light fixture	lámpara
linen	ropa blanca
linen feeder	alimentador
linen presser	planchadora
liquid	líquido
load	carga
load (of laundry)	tanda
lock	cerradura
locker	guardarropa
lotion	loción
machine	máquina
magazine	revista
matchbook	librito de cerrillos
mattress	colchón
mattress pad	cubierta del colchón
meal	comida
meat	carne
meat slicer	máquina para cortar fiambre
menu	menú
message	mensaje
microphones	micrófonos
milk	leche
mint leaves	hojas de menta
mirror	espejo
mistake	error
mixer	batidora
money	dinero
mop (dry)	trapeador seco
mop (wet)	trapeador mojado
mouse	ratón
nail	clavo
napkin	servilleta
napkin folder	dobladora de servilletas

necklace	collar
notepad	cuadernillo para notas
number	número
occurrence	ocurrencia
oil	aceite
orientation	orientación
oven	horno
pans (pots)	ollas
pans, frying	sartenes
paper towels	toallas de papel
papers	papeles / documentos
parking	estacionamiento
parking space	estacionamiento
parsley	perejil
part	parte
peeler	pelapapas
pen	pluma / lapicero
pepper (spice)	pimienta
pepper (vegetable)	pimiento
perfume	perfume
pests	animales dañinos
pillow	almohada
pillowcase	funda
pipes	cañerías
plastic bag	bolsa de plástico
platter	fuente
plumber's wrench	llave inglesa
plunger	destapador
pliers	alicates
polish, floor	lustrador de suelos
polish, furniture	cera para muebles
polisher, floor	máquina para encerar pisos
pots	ollas
pound (weight)	libra
privacy	privacidad
problem	problema
product	producto
rag	trapo
rail	barra
rat	rata
refrigerator	refrigerador
remote control	control remoto
restrooms	baños públicos
ring	anillo
roach	cucaracha

rodent	roedor
rolling pin	rodillo
room service	servicio a la habitación
rose	rosa
salad	ensalada
salt and pepper shakers	salero y pimentero
salt	sal
schedule	horario
screw	tornillo
screwdriver	destornillador
screwdriver, Phillips head	destornillador de punta de cruz
seasoning	condimento
security	seguridad
service	servicio
service entrance	entrada de servicio
service table	mesa de servicio
serving	porción
shampoo	champú
sheet	sábana
sheet folder	dobladora de sábanas
shelving unit	estante
shoes	zapatos
shower	ducha
shower cap	gorra para la ducha
shower curtain	cortina de la ducha
shrimp	camarón
sifter	tamiz
sign	letrero
silverware	cubiertos
sink (bathroom)	lavabo
sink (kitchen)	fregadero
size	tamaño
skills	habilidades
slicer	rebanadora
soap holder	jabonera
solderer	soldador
speakers	parlantes
spice	especia
spider	araña
sponge	esponja
spoon	cuchara
stain	mancha
stapler	grapadora
storage rack	estante
stove	estufa

strainer	colador / escurridor
sugar	azúcar
sugar substitute	sustituto del azúcar
sugarbowl	azucarero
suitcase	maleta
supplies	provisiones
surface	superficie
table	mesa
table linen	mantelería
table linen ironer	planchadora de mantelería
tablecloth	mantel
taxes	impuestos
tea	té
teabags	bolsitas de té
tear (rip)	rotura
telephone	teléfono
television screen	pantalla del televisor
televison set	televisor
temperature	temperatura
things	cosas
ties (for bags)	cierres
timer	reloj
tissues	pañuelos de papel
toaster	tostador
toilet	inodoro
toilet paper	papel higiénico
tool	herramienta
toolbox	caja de herramientas
top sheet	sábana de encima
towel	toalla
towel folder	dobladora de toallas
towels, paper	toallas de papel
trap	trampa
trash	basura
trash can	basurero
tray	bandeja
trolley	carrito
uniform	uniforme
utensil	utensilio
utility knife	navaja
vacuum cleaner	aspiradora
valuables	pertenencias de valor
vase	florero
vegetable	verdura / vegetal / legumbre
vent	escape

English-Spanish Glossary

vinegar	vinagre
vise grips	pinzas perras
wages	sueldo
washer (for bolt)	arandela
watch	reloj
water	agua
wax	cera
wet mop	trapeador mojado
window	ventana
window pane	vidrio
window sills	repisas
wiring	instalación eléctrica
wrench	llave
wrench, plumber's	llave inglesa
wrinkle	arruga
yolk	yema

Glosario español-inglés

Expresiones

Adiós.	Good-bye.
¿Adónde... ?	Where to . . . ?
Bienvenido.	Welcome.
Buenas noches.	Good night.
Buenas tardes.	Good afternoon.
Buenas tardes. / noches.	Good evening.
Buenos días.	Good morning.
¿Cómo... ?	How . . . ?
¿Cómo está usted?	How are you?
¿Cómo se dice... ?	How do you say . . . ?
¿Con quién... ?	Who with . . . ?
¿Cuál... ?	What . . . ?
¿Cuándo... ?	When . . . ?
¿Cuánto... ?	How much . . . ?
¿Cuántos... ?	How many . . . ?
Cuidado. / Tenga cuidado.	Be careful.
¿De dónde... ?	Where from . . . ?
de la mañana	A.M.
de la tarde / de la noche	P.M.
De nada.	You're welcome.
¿De quién... ?	Whose . . . ?
Disculpe.	Excuse me.
¿Dónde... ?	Where . . . ?
Gracias.	Thank you.
¿Hasta cuándo... ?	Until when . . . ?
Hasta luego.	See you later.
Hola.	Hello.
Llame al nueve-uno-uno.	Call 911.
Lo siento.	I'm sorry.
No.	No.

No...	Don't . . .
¡Ojalá!	God willing!
¿Para qué... ?	What for . . . ?
¿Por cuánto tiempo... ?	For how long . . . ?
Por favor.	Please.
¿Por qué?	Why . . . ?
¿Qué... ?	How . . . ?
¿Qué... ?	What . . . ?
¿Quién... ?	Who . . . ?
Sí.	Yes.

Personas

alguien	someone
amigo, amiga	friend
ayudante de mesero	buser
cocinero /cocinera	cook
él	he
ella	she
ellos / ellas	they
empleado (-a), (-os), (-as)	employees
encargado del servicio de mantenimiento	maintenance man / engineer
esposa	wife
esposo	husband
hermana	sister
hermano	brother
hija	daughter
hijo	son
hijos / hijas	children (sons and daughters)
huésped	guest
ingeniero	maintenance man / engineer
jefe	boss
la, le, a ella	her
lavandero / lavandera	laundry worker
lavaplatos	dishwasher
lo, le, a él	him
mamá / madre	mother
niño, niña	child
niños, niñas	children
nosotros / nosotras	we
novia	girlfriend
novio	boyfriend
padres	parents

papá / padre	father
patrón	boss
persona importante	VIP
personal	staff / employees
personal para la cocina	kitchen staff
personal para la limpieza	cleaning staff
referencia	reference
usted	you
ustedes	you all
vecino, vecina	neighbor
yo	I

Lugares

áreas públicas	public areas
armario	closet (storage)
armario para la ropa blanca	closet (linen)
baño	bathroom
cocina	kitchen
comedor	dining room
cuarto de recreo	playroom
cuarto	bedroom
despensa	pantry
dormitorio	bedroom
entrada de servicio	service entrance
garaje	garage
gimnasio	gym
guardarropa	closet (clothes)
habitación	room
habitación para huéspedes	guest room
hotel	hotel
lavandería	laundry room
lobby	lobby
lugar	place
parada de autobuses	bus stop
pasillo	hall
piscina	swimming pool
piso	floor (of a building)
puerta de atrás	back door
puerta principal	front door
recámara	bedroom
restaurante	restaurant
sótano	basement
suite	suite

Palabras que describen las personas, las cosas y los lugares

(Note: the endings of these words may change to match the gender or number of the words they describe)

abierto (-a), (-os), (-as)	open / unlocked
alto (-a), (-os), (-as)	high
antiguo (-a), (-os), (-as)	old
atento (-a), (-os), (-as)	attentive
bajo (-a), (-os), (-as)	low
bajos	flat (shoes)
blanco (-a), (-os), (-as)	white
bloqueado (-a), (-os), (-as)	blocked / stopped up
bueno (-a), (-os), (-as)	good
caliente, calientes	hot (water, food, etc.)
calor, hace	it's hot
cárnico (-a), (-os), (-as)	meat (products)
cerrado (-a), (-os), (-as) con llave	locked
cómodo (-a), (-os), (-as)	comfortable
con suela de hule	rubber-soled (shoes)
contratado (-a), (-os), (-as)	hired
cordial, cordiales	courteous
crudo (-a), (-os), (-as)	raw
dañado (-a), (-os), (-as)	damaged
de cinco estrellas	five-star
de goma	rubber
de hule	rubber
de madera	wooden
despedido (-a), (-os), (-as)	fired (from a job)
doblado (-a), (-os), (-as)	folded
doble	double
eficiente	efficient
en buen orden	presentable
enfermo (-a), (-os), (-as)	sick
entero (-a), (-os), (-as)	whole
especial	special / VIP
extraño (-a), (-os), (-as)	strange
fino (-a), (-os), (-as)	fine (small) / thin (slices)
fresco (-a), (-os), (-as)	fresh
frío (-a), (-os), (-as)	cold
fuerte, fuertes	sturdy
grande, grandes	big

Glosario español-inglés

grueso (-a), (-os), (-as)	thick
hace calor	it's hot (weather)
hace sol	it's sunny
hace viento	it's windy
húmedo (-a), (-os), (-as)	damp
importante, importantes	important
innecesario (-a), (-os), (-as)	unnecessary
interior	interior
limpiado en seco	dry-cleaned
limpio (-a), (-os), (-as)	clean
malo (-a), (-os), (-as)	bad
medio alta	medium (temperature)
menor, menores	minor
mojado (-a), (-os), (-as)	wet
muerto (-a), (-os), (-as)	dead
necesario (-a), (-os), (-as)	necessary
no bloqueado (-a), (-os), (-as)	clear (drain)
nublado	cloudy
nuevo (-a), (-os), (-as)	new
oscuro (-a), (-os), (-as)	dark
peligroso (-a), (-os), (-as)	unsafe
pequeño (-a), (-os), (-as)	small
personal, personales	personal
pesado (-a), (-os), (-as)	heavy
preparado (-a), (-os), (-as)	prepared
primordial	vital
puntual, puntuales	punctual
quemada	burned-out (bulb)
resbaloso (-a), (-os), (-as)	slippery
roto (-a), (-os), (-as)	broken
saludable	healthy
seco (-a), (-os), (-as)	dry
sencilla	single (room)
serio (-a), (-os), (-as)	serious
sol, hace	it's sunny
sucio (-a), (-os), (-as)	dirty
tapizado (-a), (-os), (-as)	upholstered
templado (-a), (-os), (-as)	cool
trancado (-a), (-os), (-as)	jammed
urgente	urgent
usado (-a), (-os), (-as)	used
vacío (-a), (-os), (-as)	empty
viejo (-a), (-os), (-as)	old
viento, hace	it's windy

Palabras que indican *cómo*

a medio camino	halfway (to a place)
bien	fine (not sick) / well (satisfactorily)
buen tiempo	fine (weather)
con cortesía	courteously
con cuidado	carefully
en seguida	immediately / promptly
frecuentemente	frequently
lentamente	slowly
más o menos	so-so
por separado	separately
sin ruido	quietly

Palabras que indican *cuándo*

adelantado, por	in advance
ahora	now
cuanto antes	promptly, right away
en punto	on the dot
hasta	until
hoy	today
más tarde	later
medianoche, a	at midnight
mediodía, a	at noon
mientras	while
nunca	never
pronto	soon
puntual	on time
siempre	always
temprano	early
todos los días	every day

Palabras que indican *cuánto* o *cuántos*

demasiado	too many, too much
dos veces	two times
muchas veces	many times
muchos	many
poco	little (amount)
un poco	a little

una vez	one time
unos pocos	a few
varios	several

Palabras que indican *dónde*

a casa	home
a la derecha	right (direction)
a la izquierda	left (direction)
abajo	down there, downstairs
afuera	outside
ahí	there
al lado de	next to
allí	over there
aquí	here
arriba	up there, upstairs
cerca	near
debajo de	underneath
delante de	in front of
dentro	inside
dentro de	inside
detrás de	in back of / behind
en	in / on / at
en casa	at home
encima de	on top of
entre	between
fuera de	out of
lejos	far
por	through
por debajo de	under

Palabras que indican *de quién*

mi, mis	my
mío	mine
nuestro	our, ours
propio	one's own
su, sus	your, his, her, their
suyo	yours, his, hers, theirs

Palabras pequeñas

a	to
antes	before
así	like this / like that
con	with
conmigo	with me
depende	depending
en	in, on, at
esas, esos	those
ese, esa	that
estas, estos	these
este, esta	this
extra	extra
por	per / through
porque	because
primero	first
primordial	most important
quizás	maybe
si	if
sin	without
solo	alone

Actividades

abrir	open
abrir la llave del agua	turn on (water)
administrar	administer
adobar	marinate
agacharse	bend
agarrar	grab
agregar	add (to something)
aguantar	tolerate / stand
airear	air out
ajustar	adjust
alimentar	feed
alisar	smooth
añadir	add (to something)
anotar	record (in a ledger)
apagar	turn off (electrical)
apilar	stack
apretar	push (a button)
arreglar	arrange / fix / make (bed)
arrodillar	kneel

Glosario español-inglés

asar a la parrilla	broil
asegurarse	make sure
aumentar	raise
ayudar	assist / help
barrer	sweep
batir	beat (eggs, batter)
beber	drink
buscar	go get / look for
caerse	fall
cambiar	change / replace
cargar	load
cerrar	close / draw (curtains)
cerrar con llave	lock
cerrar la llave del agua	turn off (water)
checar	check / inspect / monitor
cocinar en el horno	bake / roast
colgar	hang
colocar	place
contactar	contact
contratar	hire
correr	run (go fast)
cortar	chop / cut
dar	give
decir	tell
decorar	garnish
dejar	leave (something)
dejar en adobo	marinate
dejar en el refrigerador	refrigerate
dejar que	let (allow)
dejar que se enfríe	cool
derramar	spill
descongelar	defrost
desenredar	untangle
despedir	fire (from a job)
devolver	return (something)
distribuir	distribute
doblar	fold
empacar	pack
empezar	start
empujar	push
encender	light (candles) / turn on
encontrar	find
enfermarse	get sick
enmasillar	caulk
enseñar	show how to / teach

Glosario español-inglés

entender	understand
entrar	come in / enter
envolver	wrap
escribir su nombre	sign in / sign out
espaciar	space
esperar	expect / wait
estar en marcha	run (a machine)
estirar	roll (dough)
estofar	braise
fijarse en	monitor
firmar	sign / sign in / sign out
fregar	scrub
freír	fry
fumar	smoke
girar	turn
guardar	keep
guiar	guide
hacer	do / make
hacer inspecciones	inspect
hacer reparaciones	make repairs
hacer ruido	rattle
hervir	boil
informar	report
instalar	install
ir	go
jalar	pull
lastimarse	get hurt
lavar	wash
levantar	lift
limpiar	clean / clear / wipe
limpiar en seco	dry-clean
limpiar las manchas	spot-clean
llamar	call
llegar	arrive
llenar	fill
llevar	carry / take (to a place) / wear
lustrar	polish (furniture)
mandar	send
mantener	maintain
marcar	mark
medir	measure
meter	insert
meter debajo	tuck in (a sheet)
mezclar	mix
mezclar bien	cream (butter)

Glosario español-inglés

mostrar	show
necesitar	need
observar	observe / watch
operar	operate
ordenar	order
organizar	organize
pagar	pay
parar	stop
pasar	transfer
pasar el trapeador	mop
pasar la aspiradora	vacuum
pasarle el trapo por	wipe / dust
pedir	ask for
pelar	peel
perder	drop / lose
pesar	weigh
poner	put / set (table) / set up (tables)
poner atención	be attentive
poner en marcha	start to operate
preguntar	ask (a question)
preparar	prepare
proporcionar	provide
pulir	polish / shine (metal)
quemar	burn
quitar	remove
reciclar	recycle
recoger	pick up / retrieve
reemplazar	replace
rellenar	refill
remover	stir
reparar	repair
reportar	report
resbalarse	slip
retirar	remove (plates)
romper	break
sacar	take off / take out
salir de	leave (a place)
salpicar	spray
seguir	follow
seleccionar	set
separar	separate / sort
ser cordial	be courteous
servir	serve
soltar	loosen
tamizar	sift

tener	have
tener cuidado	be careful
tener un accidente	have an accident
terminar	finish
tirar	throw
tocar	ring (bell) / touch
tocar a la puerta	knock
tomar	drink / take
trabajar	work
traer	bring
trancarse	jam
tratar con cortesía	be courteous
untar (mantequilla)	spread (butter)
usar	use / wear
vaciar	empty
venir	come
ver	see
verter	pour

Cosas

accidente	accident
aceite	oil
acondicionador de aire	air conditioner
actitud	attitude
agua	water
agujero	hole
alcohol	alcohol
alfombra	carpet
alicates	pliers
alimentador	linen feeder
almohada	pillow
altura	height
ambulancia	ambulance
anillo	ring
animales dañinos	pests
arandela	washer (for bolt)
araña	spider
área	area
aretes	earrings
arruga	wrinkle
artículo	item
ascensor	elevator
aspiradora	vacuum cleaner

Glosario español-inglés

ayuda	assistance / help
azúcar	sugar
azucarero	sugarbowl
bandeja	tray
banquete	banquet
bañera	bathtub
baños públicos	restrooms
barra	bar (for drinks) / rail
basura	trash / garbage
basurero	trash can
batidor	blender
batidora	mixer
bolsa	bag
bolsa de plástico	plastic bag
bolsa del filtro	filter bag
bombilla	light bulb
botón	button
botones de control	controls
burro de planchar	ironing board
café	coffee
cafetera	coffee maker
caja	box
caja de herramientas	toolbox
cajones	drawers
calefacción	heating unit
cama	bed
camarón	shrimp
canasta	basket
candelabro	candlestick
cañerías	pipes
carga	load
carne	meat
carretilla	cart
carrito	cart / trolley
categoría	category
celular	cell phone
cenicero	ashtray
cera	wax
cera para muebles	furniture polish
cerradura	lock
cesta	basket
champú	shampoo
cheque	check
chocolates	chocolates
cierres	ties

Glosario español-inglés

cinta de alimentación	feeder ribbon
cinta transportadora	conveyor belt
clara	egg white
clavo	nail
colador	colander / strainer
colchón	mattress
collar	necklace
comida	food / meal
cómoda	bureau
condiciones	conditions
condimento	seasoning
congelador	freezer
control remoto	remote control
copa	glass (wine)
cortina	curtain
cortina de la ducha	shower curtain
cortinas gruesas	drapes
cosas	things
crema	cream
cuadernillo para notas	notepad
cubeta	bucket
cubierta del colchón	mattress pad
cubiertos	silverware
cubrecama	bedspread
cuchara	spoon
cuchillo	knife
cucaracha	cockroach
dedo	finger
delantal	apron
desagües	drains
descanso	break (rest)
destapador	plunger
destornillador	screwdriver
destornillador de punta de cruz	Phillips head screwdriver
destribuidor	distributor
detergente	detergent
dinero	money
dobladora	folding machine
dobladora de frazadas	blanket folder
dobladora de sábanas	sheet folder
dobladora de servilletas	napkin folder
dobladora de toallas	towel folder
documentos	documents / official papers
drogas	drugs
ducha	shower

Glosario español-inglés

efectivo	cash
ensalada	salad
entrada	entrance
entrada de servicio	service entrance
equipo	equipment
error	mistake
escalera de mano	ladder
escape	vent
especia	spice
espejo	mirror
esponja	sponge
estacionamiento	parking space / parking
estante	shelving unit / storage rack
estufa	stove
filtro	filter
florero	vase
folleto	brochure
frazada	blanket
fregadero	kitchen sink
frutas	fruit
fuente	platter
funda	pillowcase
galletas	cookies
gorra para la ducha	shower cap
grapadora	stapler
grasa	fat / grease
guantes	gloves
guardarropa	closet / locker
guarnición	garnish
habilidades	skills
harina	flour
herramienta	tool
hierbas	herbs
hojas de menta	mint leaves
horario	schedule
hormiga	ant
horno	oven
huellas dactilares	fingerprints
huevo	egg
impuestos	taxes
indicador	dial
ingredientes	ingredients
inodoro	toilet
insecticida	insecticide
insectos	insects

Glosario español-inglés

instalación eléctrica	wiring
instrucciones	instructions
jabonera	soap holder
joyas	jewelry
lámpara	lamp / light fixture
lapicero	pen
lavabo	bathroom sink
lavandería	laundry / laundry room
lavaplatos	dishwasher
leche	milk
legumbre	vegetable
lejía	bleach
letrero	sign
libra	pound (weight)
librito de cerrillos	matchbook
libro	book
limón, trozos de	lemon wedges
limpiador de desagües	drain cleaner
limpiadores	cleaning supplies
líquido	liquid
llave	key / wrench
llave inglesa	plumber's wrench
loción	lotion
loción para el cuerpo	body lotion
lustrador de suelos	floor polish
luz	light / electricity
maleta	suitcase
mancha	stain
manos	hands
mantel	tablecloth
mantelería	table linen
mantequilla	butter
mantequillera	butter dish
máquina	machine
máquina para cortar fiambre	meat slicer
máquina para encerar pisos	floor polisher
martillo	hammer
masa	batter / dough
masilla	caulking
mensaje	message
menú	menu
mesa	table
mesa de servicio	service table
micrófonos	microphones
migas de pan	breadcrumbs

Glosario español-inglés

molde	baking pan
muebles	furniture
navaja	utility knife
número	number
ocurrencia	occurrence
ollas	cooking pots
orientación	orientation
pantalla del televisor	television screen
pañuelos de papel	tissues
papel higiénico	toilet paper
papeles	official papers / documents
parlantes	speakers
parte	part
pastel	cake
pelapapas	peeler
perejil	parsley
perfume	perfume
perilla	doorknob
pertenencias	belongings
pertenencias de valor	valuables
pescado	fish
picadora	chopper
pie de la cama	foot of the bed
pimienta	pepper (spice)
pimiento	pepper (vegetable)
pinzas perras	vise grips
piso	floor / floor (of a building)
pista de baile	dance floor
plancha	iron
planchadora	linen presser / ironer
planchadora de mantelería	table linen ironer
plataforma para la banda	bandstand
plato	dish / plate
pluma	pen
porción	serving
postre	dessert
primeros auxilios	first aid
privacidad	privacy
problema	problem
productos	products / supplies
programa	cycle (of machine)
puerta	door
puerta de atrás	back door
puerta principal	front door
pulsera	bracelet

Glosario español-inglés

punta	corner (of a sheet)
químicas	chemical supplies
rallador	grater
rata	rat
ratón	mouse
rebanadora	slicer
recuerdo	favor (party)
redecilla	hairnet
refrigerador	refrigerator
reloj	clock / watch / timer
repisas	window sills
restos de comida	garbage
revista	magazine
rodillo	rolling pin
roedor	rodent
ropa	clothing
ropa blanca	linen
ropa de cama	bedding
rosa	rose
rotura	tear (rip)
sábana	sheet
sábana de abajo	bottom sheet
sábana de encima	top sheet
sal	salt
salero y pimentero	salt and pepper shakers
sangre	blood
sartenes	frying pans
secador	dryer (for hair)
secadora	dryer (for clothes)
seguridad	security
servicio	service
servicio a la habitación	room service
servicio de lavandería	laundry service
servilleta	napkin
silla	chair
sillón	easy chair
sistema de calefacción	heating system
soldador	solderer
suavizante de telas	fabric softener
sueldo	wages
suelo	floor
superficie	surface
sustituto de la crema	creamer
sustituto del azúcar	sugar substitute
taladro	drill

Glosario español-inglés

tamaño	size
tamiz	sifter
tanda	load (of laundry)
tapa	lid
tapete del baño	bathmat
tarjeta	card
taza	cup
té	tea
tela	fabric
teléfono	telephone
televisor	televison set
temperatura	temperature
tenedor	fork
timbre	doorbell
toalla	towel
toallas de papel	paper towels
tornillo	screw
tostador	toaster
trabajo	job
trampa	trap
trapeador mojado	wet mop
trapeador seco	dry mop
trapo	rag
trozo	chunk / wedge
uniforme	uniform
utensilio	utensil
vajilla	china
vaso	glass (drinking)
vegetal	vegetable
vela	candle
ventana	window
verdura	vegetable
vidrio	window pane
vinagre	vinegar
yema	egg yolk
zapatos	shoes
zócalos	baseboards